Writer's Companion

Support and Practice for Writing

Grade 2

Contents

Introduction

When you first learn a new game, you usually are not very good at it. The more you play, the better you can become.

You can also get better at writing by doing it. This book will help you become the best writer you can be.

The Writing Process

Writing is a process in which you go through different steps. The writing process is often divided into five steps.

Prewriting

In this step, you plan what you're going to write. You pick a topic and brainstorm ideas about it. You think of a good order for the ideas.

Drafting

In this step, you put your ideas in sentences and paragraphs. Follow your Prewriting plan to write a first draft.

Revising

In this step, you make your writing clearer and stronger.

Proofreading

In this step, you check for mistakes in grammar, spelling, capitalization, and punctuation. Make a final, neat copy of your composition.

Publishing

Last, you pick a way to present your work to others. You may want to add pictures, make a class book, or read your work aloud.

Writer's Craft and Writing Traits

Good writing takes special skills and strategies. This web shows the traits, or characteristics, of good writing. You'll learn much more about these traits in this book.

The Traits of Good Writing

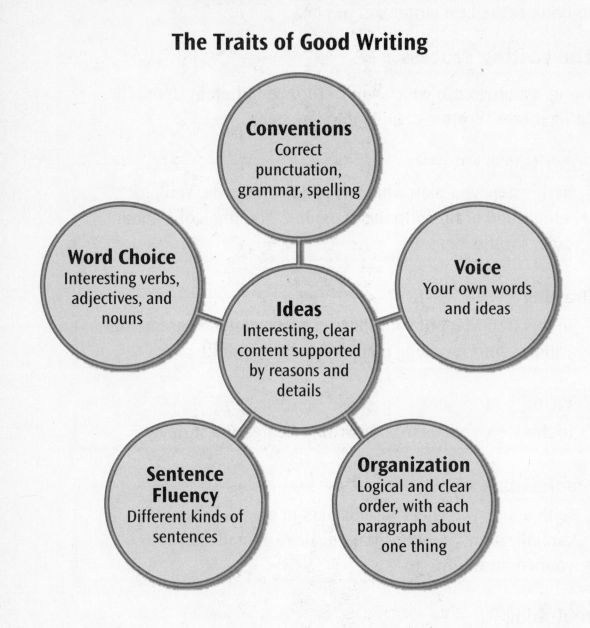

Conventions
Correct punctuation, grammar, spelling

Word Choice
Interesting verbs, adjectives, and nouns

Ideas
Interesting, clear content supported by reasons and details

Voice
Your own words and ideas

Sentence Fluency
Different kinds of sentences

Organization
Logical and clear order, with each paragraph about one thing

© Harcourt

Traits Checklist

As you practice writing, ask yourself these questions.

☑ **FOCUS/IDEAS**	Do I stay on the topic? Do I use details to support my ideas?
☑ **ORGANIZATION**	Do I have a beginning, a middle, and an ending? Are my ideas grouped in paragraphs?
☑ **VOICE**	Do I use my own words and ideas? Do I seem to care about my topic and my audience?
☑ **WORD CHOICE**	Do I use specific words and colorful words?
☑ **SENTENCE FLUENCY**	Do I use different kinds of sentences?
☑ **CONVENTIONS**	Are my spelling, grammar, and punctuation correct?

Writer's Companion
Introduction

Name _____

Look at Topics and Ideas

When writers choose a **topic**, it is the main idea they want to focus on. The **ideas** are the things they want to tell readers about the topic.

A. Read the following model. Find the topic in the first sentence. Find the ideas in the other sentences.

Literature Model

On a shiny green leaf sat a small green chameleon.

It moved onto a brown tree and turned brownish.

Then it rested on a red flower and turned reddish.

When the chameleon moved slowly across the yellow

sand, it turned yellowish. You could hardly see it.

—from *The Mixed-Up Chameleon*
by Eric Carle

B. Look for the topic and ideas.

   1. Circle the word that names the topic.

   2. Underline two ideas about the topic.

C. Explain why it was hard to see the chameleon.

_____

_____

_____

© Harcourt

Name _____

Explore Topics and Ideas

The topic is the main idea. Other ideas are points the writer wants to make about the main idea. Other ideas are also messages the writer wants to tell the reader.

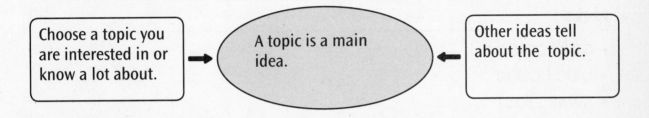

A. Circle the topic. Then underline ideas about the topic.

Example (I like my pants.) My pants are blue. They have pockets.

1. Flowers bloom in the spring. There are yellow daffodils. There are pink tulips.

2. We have two rabbits. The rabbits live in our house. They are quiet pets.

3. Do you like pizza? Pizza is hot. Pizza has cheese.

B. Circle the topic sentence. Underline the idea sentences. Cross out the idea sentence that does not fit with the topic.

The wind blew and blew. It rattled the windows. Leaves blew off the tree. The baby laughed.

C. Topic: The baby laughed. Write an idea sentence about this on the line.

Idea Sentence: _____

_____

9

Name _____

Use Topics and Ideas

Write down a topic that you know. Then list some ideas about it. Here is how one student wrote about a fish.

Example **Name of Topic:** _fish_____

Ideas
• gold color • blue house • swims fast

A. Think about something you like. Then fill out the chart.

Name of Topic: _____

Ideas
•

B. Use your chart. Write a topic sentence and some ideas about your topic.

_____

_____

_____

_____

_____

© Harcourt

Name _____

The Parts of a Topic and Idea List

Below is a Topic and Idea List. As you read, think about the topic and the ideas. Then answer the questions.

Student Model

DRAFT

My Fish Mikey
by Ramon

Topic: Fish

Idea: A fish in a bowl

My fish is gold.

My fish has a tail.

It lives in a bowl.

A cat has fur.

It swims so fast!

It hides in its blue house.

> Look for the **topic** in the first sentence.

> Tell one **idea** about the topic.

> Idea

> Idea

> Idea

> Tell another **idea** about the topic.

1. What is the writing about? Underline the topic.

2. What is one idea about the topic? Put a box around the idea.

3. Which sentence is not about the topic? Circle the sentence.

Writer's Grammar
An exclamation point (!) is used to show strong feeling. Find an example of an exclamation in the Student Model.

Name _____

Evaluate a Topic and Idea List

When you evaluate a Topic and Idea List, ask yourself
these questions:

- Can you tell what the topic is?

- Are all the ideas about the same topic?

A. Reread the Student Model on page 11. Then answer these questions.

   1. What is this information mostly about?

   _____

   2. What are some important ideas the writer shares with readers?

   _____

   _____

B. Now evaluate the Student Model. Put a check in the box next to each
thing the writer has done well. If you do not think the writer did a good
job with something, do not check the box.

    ☐ The writer told the topic in the first sentence.
    ☐ The writer told ideas about only one topic.

C. How do you think the writer could make the topic and idea list better?
Write your ideas below.

_____

_____

© Harcourt

See the rubric on page 207 for another
way to evaluate the Student Model.

Name _____

Revise by Adding Ideas

One thing the writer could have done better is to add more
ideas about the topic. Here is an example of an idea that could
be added to the list.

Example I feed my fish after school.

A. Revise the Student Model by adding sentences with ideas
about fish. Use the Word Bank for ideas.

Word Bank

some
big
small
swim
ocean
back and forth
_____
_____

1. _____

_____

_____

2. _____

_____

_____

B. Revise your writing on page 10. Add some idea sentences about
your topic.

_____

_____

_____

_____

_____

Name _____

Look at Adding Details

Writers add **details** to sentences. Details give more information about a topic.

A. Read the model. Look for details about the girl.

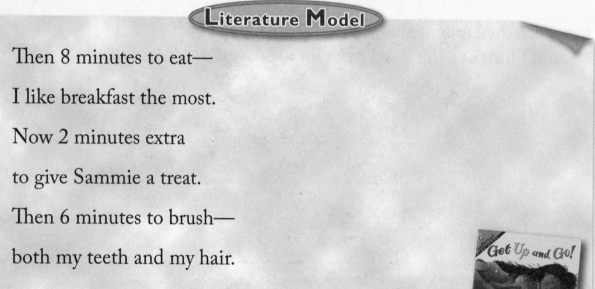

Literature Model

Then 8 minutes to eat—

I like breakfast the most.

Now 2 minutes extra

to give Sammie a treat.

Then 6 minutes to brush—

both my teeth and my hair.

—from *Get Up and Go!*
by Stuart J. Murphy

B. Look for the details.

1. Circle the word that tells what the girl likes.

2. Underline the words that tell why the girl wants 2 minutes extra.

C. Explain what the girl will do in 6 minutes.

_____

_____

Name _____

Explore Adding Details

Writers add **details** to make their writing more interesting.

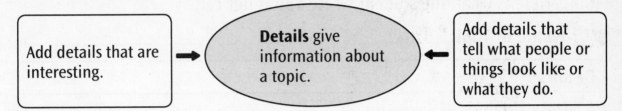

Add details that are interesting. → **Details** give information about a topic. ← Add details that tell what people or things look like or what they do.

A. Underline the details.

> **Example** The boy is wearing a <u>yellow raincoat</u>.

1. My doll has brown hair and brown eyes.

2. Look for a house with a red door.

3. I like juicy, purple plums.

B. Read this sentence from *Get Up and Go*! Underline a detail about the girl.

You're always so slow.

C. Imagine that you have a pet bird. Write two details about your bird.

_____

_____

_____

_____

Name _____

Use Adding Details

Write down a topic that you know. Then list some details about the topic. Here is what one student wrote about her cat.

Example **Name of Topic:** _cat_

Details
• black with white paws • meows a lot • plays with a ball of string

A. Think about something you know. Then fill out the chart.

Name of Topic: _____

Details

B. Write three sentences about your topic. Use your details from the chart.

_____

_____

_____

_____

_____

© Harcourt

Name _____

Detail Sentences

Detail sentences give more information about the topic. The paragraph below is a draft written by a second grader. As you read, think about the topic and the detail sentences. Then answer the questions.

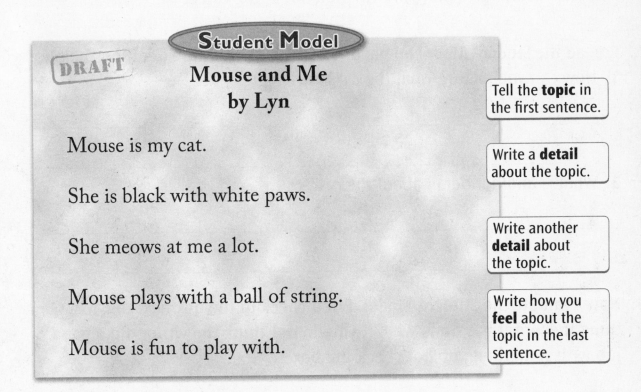

DRAFT

Student Model

Mouse and Me
by Lyn

Mouse is my cat.

She is black with white paws.

She meows at me a lot.

Mouse plays with a ball of string.

Mouse is fun to play with.

Tell the **topic** in the first sentence.

Write a **detail** about the topic.

Write another **detail** about the topic.

Write how you **feel** about the topic in the last sentence.

1. What is the writing about? Underline the topic.

2. Which sentence tells what the cat looks like? Put a box around the sentence.

3. Which sentences tell what the cat does? Circle the sentences.

Writer's Grammar
A verb is a word that shows an action. Find a verb that shows an action in the Student Model.

Name _____

Evaluate Detail Sentences

When you evaluate detail sentences, ask yourself
these questions:

- Can you tell what the topic is?
- Do all the details give more information about the topic?

A. Reread the Student Model on page 17. Then answer these questions below.

1. How can you picture what the cat looks like?

_____

_____

2. What is another detail about the cat?

_____

_____

B. Now evaluate the Student Model. Put a check in the box next to each thing the writer has done well. If you do not think the writer did a good job with something, do not check the box.

☐ The writer told the topic in the first sentence.
☐ The writer gave interesting details about the topic.

C. Do you think the writer could have done a better job? Explain how.

_____

_____

_____

See the rubric on page 207 for another
way to evaluate the Student Model.

© Harcourt

Name _____

Revise by Adding Details

One thing the writer could have done better is to add more details about the topic. Here is an example of a detail that could be added to the Student Model.

Example Mouse sleeps on my pillow.

A. Revise the Student Model by adding detail sentences about Mouse, the cat. Use the Word Bank for ideas.

1. _____

   _____

2. _____

   _____

Word Bank

beautiful

green

eyes

tuna

favorite

_____

_____

B. Revise your writing on page 16. Add a detail sentence about your topic.

_____

_____

_____

_____

_____

_____

_____

_____

_____

Name _____

Look at Main Idea and Detail Sentences

The **main idea** is the topic. **Detail sentences** tell more about the topic.

A. Read the following model. Find the main idea. Then find the detail sentences about the main idea.

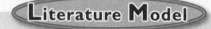
Literature Model

In the fall,
Henry and his big dog Mudge
took long walks in the woods.
Henry loved looking at
the tops of the trees.
He liked the leaves:
orange, yellow, brown, and red.

—from *Henry and Mudge
Under the Yellow Moon*
by Cynthia Rylant

B. Look for the main idea and detail sentences.

1. Circle the main idea.

2. Underline one detail sentence about the main idea.

C. What did Henry like about the leaves?

_____

_____

_____

© Harcourt

Name _____

Explore Main Idea and Detail Sentences

The **main idea** is found in the **topic sentence**. The **detail sentences** give information about the main idea.

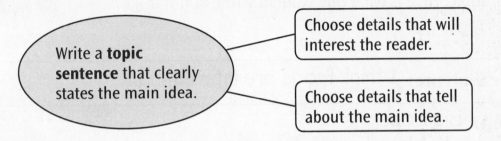

Write a **topic sentence** that clearly states the main idea.

Choose details that will interest the reader.

Choose details that tell about the main idea.

A. Put a box around the topic sentence. Underline the detail sentences.

Example | I made a mask. | The mask is a tiger's face. It has stripes.

1. The sun is important. The sun gives Earth light. It gives Earth heat.

2. I like crickets. Crickets chirp. They move by jumping.

B. Read these sentences from *Henry and Mudge Under the Yellow Moon*. Put a box around the topic sentence. Underline the detail sentence.

But one thing about them was the same. In the fall Henry and Mudge liked being together, most of all.

C. Why do you think Henry and Mudge liked the fall? Write one or two detail sentences on the lines.

_____

_____

_____

_____

© Harcourt

Name _____

Use Main Idea and Detail Sentences

The main idea is the topic. It is found in the topic sentence. Choose a topic you know. Write a topic sentence. Then list details about your topic. Here is what one student wrote about frogs.

Example

Topic Sentence:	I think frogs are interesting.
Details:	big leaps stick heads out of water croaking at night

A. Think about something you know. Then fill out the chart.

Topic Sentence:
Details:

B. Write your topic sentence and two detail sentences about your topic. Use ideas from your chart.

_____

_____

_____

_____

_____

 © Harcourt

Name _____

The Parts of a Paragraph

A **paragraph** is about one topic. The paragraph below is a draft written by a second grader. As you read, think about the topic and the detail sentences. Then answer the questions.

Student Model

DRAFT

Frogs in the Pond
by Willie

I think frogs are interesting. They can take really big leaps! I see frogs stick their heads out of the water. I hear frogs croaking in the pond at night.

> Tell the **topic** in the first sentence.

> Write a **detail** about the topic.

> Write another **detail** about the topic.

> Write one more **detail** about the topic.

1. What is the main idea of the writing? Underline the topic sentence.

2. What information does the second sentence give about the topic? Circle the detail.

3. What is another detail about the topic? Circle the detail sentence.

4. On the lines, write one more new detail sentence about frogs.

_____

_____

Writer's Grammar

The first line of a paragraph is indented. This means it starts a few spaces in. Find the paragraph indent in the Student Model.

Name _____

Evaluate a Paragraph

When you evaluate a paragraph, ask yourself these questions:

- Can you tell what the main idea is?
- Are all the details about the same topic?

A. Reread the Student Model on page 23. Then answer these questions.

1. How do you know what the paragraph is about?

_____

2. Why does the writer think frogs are interesting?

_____

_____

B. Now evaluate the Student Model. Put a check in the box next to each thing the writer has done well. If you do not think the writer did a good job with something, do not check the box.

☐ The writer told what the paragraph is about in a topic sentence.
☐ The writer gave interesting information in detail sentences.
☐ The writer included details about only one topic.

C. How do you think the writer could make the paragraph better? Write your ideas below.

_____

_____

_____

© Harcourt

See the rubric on page 207 for another way to evaluate the Student Model.

Name _____

Revise by Adding Interesting Details

One thing the writer could have done better is to add interesting details about the topic. Here is an example of a detail sentence that could be added to the Student Model.

Example Frogs sit on plants on top of the water.

A. Revise the Student Model by adding interesting detail sentences about frogs. Use the Word Bank for ideas.

1. _____

_____

2. _____

_____

3. _____

_____

Word Bank

insects
webbed
feet
colors
green
brown
_____
_____

B. Revise your writing on page 22. Add some new detail sentences about your topic.

_____

_____

_____

_____

_____

_____

_____

© Harcourt

Writer's Companion • UNIT 1
Lesson 3 *Main Idea and Detail Sentences*

Name _____

Review Ideas

Writers tell the main idea of their writing in a topic sentence.
They tell details about the main idea in other sentences.

A. Read the following Literature Model. Look for the main idea and details.

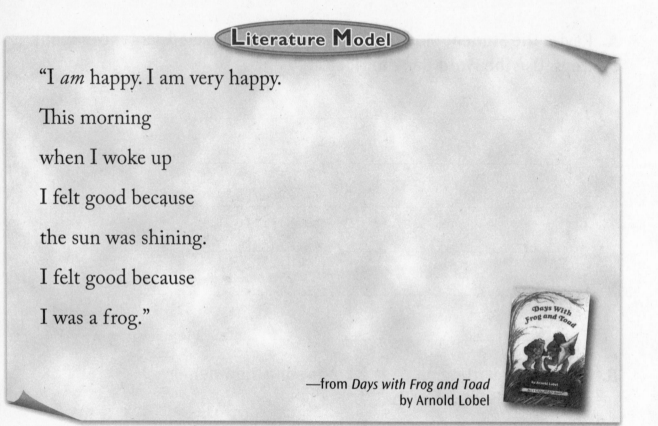

Literature Model

"I *am* happy. I am very happy.

This morning

when I woke up

I felt good because

the sun was shining.

I felt good because

I was a frog."

—from *Days with Frog and Toad*
by Arnold Lobel

B. Look for the main idea and detail sentences.

   1. Put a box around the topic sentence that has the main idea.

   2. Underline one detail about the topic.

C. When did Frog feel good?

_____

Name _____

Review Ideas

Writers add details to make their stories more interesting.

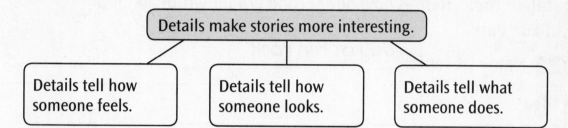

A. **Read the following Literature Model. Look for interesting details.**

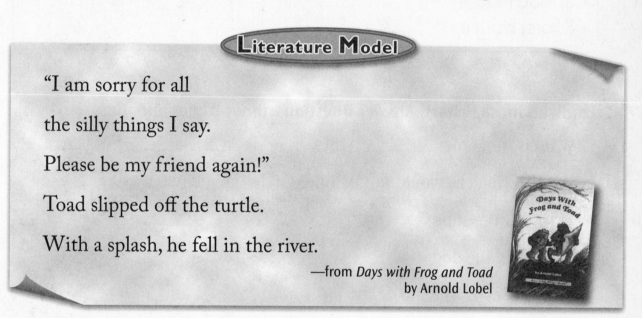

Literature Model

"I am sorry for all

the silly things I say.

Please be my friend again!"

Toad slipped off the turtle.

With a splash, he fell in the river.

—from *Days with Frog and Toad*
by Arnold Lobel

B. **Answer the question. Write the detail.**

Example The girl was glad it snowed. She made a snow person.

Which detail tells how someone felt? _____

Which detail tells what someone did? _____

1. Which detail in the model tells how someone felt? _____

2. Which detail in the model tells what someone did?

_____

_____

Writer's Companion • UNIT 1
Lesson 4 *Review Ideas*

Name _____

Review Ideas

Writers choose a topic they know. Then they write down ideas about their topic. Here is how one second grader wrote about a day at Fun Park.

Example **Name of Topic:** _Day at Fun Park_ _____

Ideas
• wild animal bus • space ride • Scary House

A. **Think about the chart. Answer questions about topics and ideas.**

1. What is the topic: _____

2. Which two ideas would not belong? Circle the ideas.

- wild water slide

- feeding the dog

- giant Ferris wheel

- ice cream stand

- dragon roller coaster

- brush my teeth

B. **Write an interesting topic sentence for Day at Fun Park.**

_____

_____

_____

_____

Name _____

The Parts of a Paragraph

A **paragraph** has a topic sentence that tells the main idea. It has detail sentences that tell about the main idea. Below is a draft written by a second grader. As you read, think about the main idea and details. Then answer the questions.

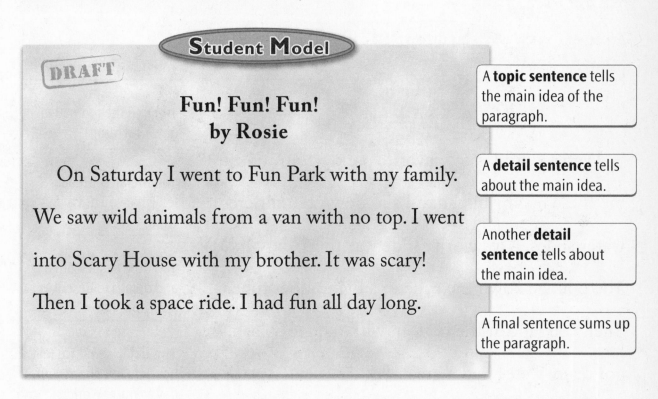

Student Model

DRAFT

Fun! Fun! Fun!
by Rosie

On Saturday I went to Fun Park with my family.

We saw wild animals from a van with no top. I went into Scary House with my brother. It was scary!

Then I took a space ride. I had fun all day long.

> A **topic sentence** tells the main idea of the paragraph.

> A **detail sentence** tells about the main idea.

> Another **detail sentence** tells about the main idea.

> A final sentence sums up the paragraph.

1. What is the main idea of the paragraph? Underline the topic sentence.

2. What detail in the second sentence is interesting? Circle the detail.

3. Which sentence tells you how the writer feels about a day at Fun Park? Circle this detail sentence.

Writer's Grammar
The word *I* is always written as a capital letter. Find the word *I* in the Student Model. Look for an *I* that is not at the beginning of a sentence.

Name _____

Evaluate a Paragraph

A. Two more children wrote a paragraph about a day at a park. The
paragraph below got a score of 4. A score of 4 means excellent.
As you read, think about the teacher's notes.

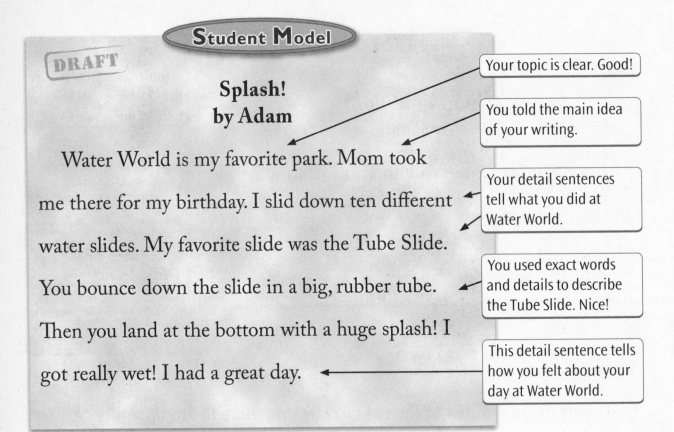

Student Model

DRAFT

Splash!
by Adam

Water World is my favorite park. Mom took

me there for my birthday. I slid down ten different

water slides. My favorite slide was the Tube Slide.

You bounce down the slide in a big, rubber tube.

Then you land at the bottom with a huge splash! I

got really wet! I had a great day.

Your topic is clear. Good!

You told the main idea
of your writing.

Your detail sentences
tell what you did at
Water World.

You used exact words
and details to describe
the Tube Slide. Nice!

This detail sentence tells
how you felt about your
day at Water World.

© Harcourt

Name _____

B. This paragraph got a score of 2. Why did it get a low score?

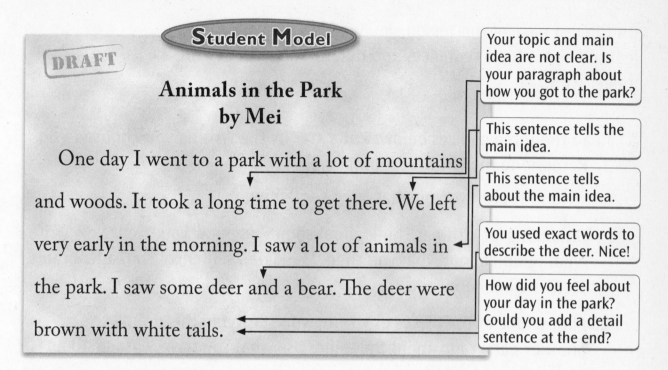

Student Model

DRAFT

Animals in the Park
by Mei

One day I went to a park with a lot of mountains and woods. It took a long time to get there. We left very early in the morning. I saw a lot of animals in the park. I saw some deer and a bear. The deer were brown with white tails.

Your topic and main idea are not clear. Is your paragraph about how you got to the park?

This sentence tells the main idea.

This sentence tells about the main idea.

You used exact words to describe the deer. Nice!

How did you feel about your day in the park? Could you add a detail sentence at the end?

C. What score would you give the student's story? Put a number on each line.

	4	3	2	1
Focus/Ideas _____	☐ The writing has a clear topic and main idea.	☐ The writing has a main idea.	☐ The topic and main idea are not very clear.	☐ The writing does not have a clear topic or main idea.
Development _____	☐ The writing has enough detail sentences to tell about each main idea.	☐ The writing has some detail sentences that tell about the main idea.	☐ The writing has a sentence that tells the main idea and one detail sentence.	☐ The writing does not have any detail sentences that tell about the main idea.
Word Choice _____	☐ The writer uses exact words and details.	☐ The writer uses some exact words and details.	☐ The writer uses only a few exact words.	☐ The writer does not use any exact words.

© Harcourt

Name _____

Extended Writing/Test Prep

On the last page of this lesson, you will use what you have learned about topic sentences and detail sentences to write a longer work.

A. Read the three choices below. Put a star by the writing you choose to do.

1. Respond to the Writing Prompt.

Writing Topic: Everyone has tried something new.

Directions for Writing: Think about something new you tried. Now write a paragraph about what you tried. Use detail sentences so readers can picture what happened.

2. Choose one of the pieces of writing you started in this unit. Write another paragraph about the topic. Use what you have learned about main idea and details.

- topic and idea list (page 11)
- detail sentences (page 17)
- paragraph (page 23)

3. Choose a new topic you would like to write about. Use detail sentences to help the reader picture what you are writing about.

B. Use the space below to plan your writing.

TOPIC: _____

TOPIC SENTENCE: _____

Name _____

C. In the space below, draw a chart that will help you plan
your writing. Fill in the chart.

NOTES

_____

_____

_____

_____

_____

_____

_____

_____

D. Write about your topic on another sheet of paper.

© Harcourt

Name _____

Answering Multiple-Choice Questions

Some writing tests have questions with answer choices. This lesson will help you practice this kind of test.

A. Some test questions may ask you about sentences. Read the test tip. Then answer the questions.

Answer questions 1–4 on the Answer Sheet below.

1. Which group of words is a **sentence**?

A Riding my bike with friends.

B When it is a warm day.

C My bike is red and black.

2. Which group of words is a **sentence**?

F It snowed all day.

G Closed our school was.

H The snow we played in.

3. Which sentence **begins** and **ends** correctly?

A we heard ducks quacking.

B Two ducks flew to the pond.

C The ducks floated on the water

4. Which sentence tells a **complete thought**?

F Had a lot of fun at the circus.

G Laughed at the clowns.

H One clown had green hair.

> **Test Tip:**
> A sentence tells a complete thought. A sentence starts with a capital letter and ends with an end mark.

Answer all test questions on this Answer Sheet.

1. Ⓐ Ⓑ Ⓒ   3. Ⓐ Ⓑ Ⓒ

2. Ⓕ Ⓖ Ⓗ   4. Ⓕ Ⓖ Ⓗ

© Harcourt

Name _____

B. Some test questions may ask you about kinds of sentences.
Read the test tip. Then answer the questions.

Answer questions 1–4 on the Answer Sheet below.

1. Which sentence is a **statement**?

   A Do you see the squirrel's nest?

   B At the top of that tall tree.

   C The nest is made of leaves.

2. Which sentence is a **question**?

   F The clouds are dark.

   G Is it going to rain?

   H Wear your raincoat.

> **Test Tip:**
> A statement ends with a period (.).
> A question ends with a question mark (?).

3. Which sentence should end with a **question mark**?

   A I like to play with your dog

   B What is your dog's name

   C Your dog caught the ball

4. Which sentence should end with a **period**?

   F Today is a very hot day

   G Can you go swimming

   H When can you go

© Harcourt

Answer all test questions on this Answer Sheet.

1. Ⓐ Ⓑ Ⓒ   3. Ⓐ Ⓑ Ⓒ

2. Ⓕ Ⓖ Ⓗ   4. Ⓕ Ⓖ Ⓗ

Name _____

C. Some test questions may ask you about sentences in a paragraph.

Read the paragraph. Read each question and mark the circle next to the correct answer. Remember to read the test tip.

Busy Bugs

(1) Do you like ants! (2) One morning I watched ants. (3) Were very busy. (4) Some ants marched in a line. (5) One ant carried a really big crumb (6) Look for ants around your house?

1. Sentence 1 should end with _____.
   - (A) a period
   - (B) a comma
   - (C) a question mark
   - (D) an exclamation point

2. Sentence 5 should end with _____.
   - (F) a capital letter
   - (G) a comma
   - (H) a question mark
   - (I) an exclamation point

> **Test Tip:**
> Be sure to read the whole paragraph first. Always reread the numbered sentence before you choose your answer.

3. Sentence 6 should end with _____.
   - (A) a period
   - (B) a comma
   - (C) a question mark
   - (D) an exclamation point

4. What is the BEST way to correct sentence 3?
   - (F) Ants very busy were.
   - (G) The ants were very busy.
   - (H) Very busy the ants were.
   - (I) Were the ants very busy?

Name _____

D. Some test questions may ask you about parts of sentences. Read the test tip. Then answer the questions.

Read the paragraph. Read each question, and mark the circle next to the correct answer.

A Class Trip

(1) My class visited a fire station. (2) All the fire trucks were yellow. (3) One truck had a big ladder. (4) We saw a very long fire hose! (5) My friend and I want to be firefighters. (6) Fighting fires is an important job.

1. What is the naming part in sentence 1?

Ⓐ My

Ⓑ My class

Ⓒ My class visited

2. What is the naming part in sentence 3?

Ⓕ One truck

Ⓖ had a big ladder

Ⓗ big ladder

3. What is the naming part in sentence 4?

Ⓐ We

Ⓑ saw

Ⓒ hose

4. What is the naming part in sentence 5?

Ⓕ My friend

Ⓖ My friend and I

Ⓗ firefighters

> **Test Tip:**
> The naming part of a sentence tells *who* or *what*. In the sentence *The little dog runs fast* the naming part is *The little dog.*

© Harcourt

Name _____

Look at Writing Dialogue

When characters speak in a story, their words are called **dialogue. Quotation marks** show where each speaker's exact words begin and end. A **comma** separates a speaker's words from other words. The word *said* tells the reader who is talking.

A. Read the following model. Notice how the writer uses quotation marks and the word *said* to show dialogue.

Literature Model

Once upon a time an old man planted a little turnip and said: "Grow, grow, little turnip, grow sweet! Grow, grow, little turnip, grow strong!"

And the turnip grew up sweet and strong and big and enormous.

—from *The Enormous Turnip*
by Alexei Tolstoy

B. Identify the dialogue.

1. Circle the quotation marks in the model.

2. Put a box around the word that tells you someone is talking.

3. Underline the words that are dialogue.

C. Who is talking in the above model?

_____

© Harcourt

Name _____

Explore Writing Dialogue

You can use **dialogue** to show what a character says.

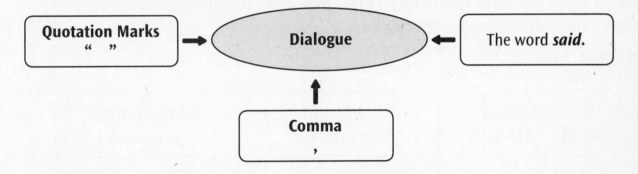

A. Read each sentence. Underline the dialogue. Circle the word *said*. Put a box around the comma that separates the dialogue from the word *said*.

Example "I'm hungry," said Caroline.

1. Simon tripped and fell. He said, "Ouch! That hurt."

2. "I can't wait to go on the trip," Andre said.

3. Maya shook her head and said, "No, thank you."

B. Read this sentence from *The Enormous Turnip*.

So the old woman called her granddaughter.

How do you know this is NOT dialogue?

_____

_____

C. Add the missing parts to the sentence below.

The old woman said That's a big turnip.

_____

_____

© Harcourt

Name _____

Use Dialogue

Before you write dialogue, first think about a topic. Next, think about what you want someone to say. Then write the dialogue. Here's how one second grader did it.

Example Topic: _Friends making a snowman_

Write dialogue and " " marks.	Use *said* and a name.	Add a comma and a period.
"Let's make a snowman" "That sounds like fun"	said Emma said Kendra	"Let's make a snowman," said Emma. "That sounds like fun," said Kendra.

A. Think about talking to a friend about something. Write the topic on the line. Then fill out the chart.

Topic: _____

Write dialogue and " " marks.	Use *said* and a name.	Add a comma and a period.

B. Use information from the chart to write two sentences of dialogue. Use another sheet of paper.

© Harcourt

Name _____

The Parts of Dialogue

Good dialogue sounds real and fits with the characters and the story.

Student Model

DRAFT

In the Snow
by Casey

Let's make a snowman!" said Emma.

"That sounds like fun!" said Kendra.

We need three balls of snow, said Emma.

"Let's use sticks for arms, said Kendra.

Emma said, "I'll get rocks for his eyes."

"His name is Harry" Kendra said.

They put a hat on his head.

Dialogue should sound real and fit with the characters and the story.

Quotation marks show which words are being spoken.

Said is a clue that you have read or will read dialogue.

Commas separate the dialogue from the word *said* and the speaker's name.

1. How do you know that Emma says she will get rocks for his eyes?

_____

_____

2. Which speaker said, "That sounds like fun"?

_____

3. Which sentence is not dialogue? Underline it.

Writer's Grammar
Dialogue and dialogue sentences have end marks. Find the end marks in the Student Model.

© Harcourt

Name _____

Evaluate Dialogue

When you evaluate dialogue, ask yourself these questions:

- Does the writer use quotation marks around the speaker's words?

- Does the writer use the word *said,* or another similar word, to show that someone is speaking?

- Does the writer use a comma to separate the dialogue from the other words in the sentence?

A. Reread the Student Model on page 41. Then use the Student Model to answer the questions below.

1. Name the two speakers in the Student Model.

_____

2. Give an example of a sentence in which the speaker's name comes after the dialogue.

_____

_____

B. Evaluate the Student Model. Check the box next to each thing the writer has done well. If the writer did not do a good job, do not check the box.

☐ The dialogue sounds real and fits with the story.
☐ The writer used quotation marks in all the right places.
☐ The writer used the word *said* and commas to separate the dialogue from the other words.

C. How do you think the writer could improve the dialogue to make it correct?

_____

_____

Writer's Companion • UNIT 2
Lesson 1 *Writing Dialogue*

42

See the rubric on page 207 for another
way to evaluate the Student Model.

© Harcourt

Name _____

Revise by Adding Commas and Quotation Marks

The writer could have done a better job of using commas and quotation marks. This is how a sentence from the Student Model can be improved.

Example "Let's use sticks for arms, said Kendra.

"Let's use sticks for arms," said Kendra.

A. Revise these sentences from the Student Model. Write them on the lines.

1. Let's make a snowman!" said Emma.

   _____

   _____

2. We need three balls of snow, said Emma.

   _____

   _____

3. "His name is Harry" Kendra said.

   _____

   _____

B. Revise both of the sentences you wrote on page 40. Try putting a speaker's name in a different place, or try using a word other than *said* to show that someone is talking.

   _____

   _____

   _____

© Harcourt

Writer's Companion • UNIT 2
Lesson 1 *Writing Dialogue*

Name _____

Look at Colorful Words

Colorful words help describe things. They make a story more interesting. Colorful words paint a picture in the reader's mind.

A. Read the following model. Look for colorful words.

Literature Model

In early spring, you can help to plant seeds in the vegetable garden. Soon they will sprout and grow into many good things to eat.

You can turn some chores into fun, like washing the car on a hot summer's day.

—from *Helping Out*
by George Ancona

B. Find the colorful words.

1. Circle a colorful word in the first paragraph.

2. Underline a colorful word in the second paragraph.

C. Rewrite this sentence. Add colorful words that help describe "many good things to eat."

Soon they will sprout and grow into many good things to eat.

_____

_____

_____

Name _____

Explore Colorful Words

Writers use **colorful words** to keep readers interested in a story. Here is how some different words can be used in place of *said*.

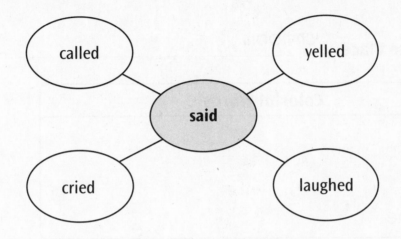

A. **Underline two colorful words in each sentence.**

Example The <u>soft</u>, <u>white</u> sand felt hot under her feet.

1. "I'm starving!" she cried, reaching for a sandwich.

2. The pretty flowers danced in the breeze.

3. The water sparkled in the bright sunshine.

B. **Rewrite this sentence to make it more interesting and colorful.**

I made a picture of a house.

_____

_____

_____

Name _____

Use Colorful Words

Colorful words make a story more interesting. Here's how one second grader planned a story about his favorite place.

Example

My Favorite Place: _Our room_

Colorful Words
giant
bright
sunshine

A. Think about your favorite place. Write its name on the line. Then fill out the chart with words to describe it.

My Favorite Place: _____

Colorful Words

B. Use the information from your chart to help you write three sentences about your favorite place.

_____

_____

_____

_____

Name _____

The Parts of a Personal Story

A personal story is about the writer. Colorful words add interest and details to the story.

Student Model

DRAFT

Our Room
by Paul

Pete and I wanted to repaint our room. It was plain and white. Mom said we could pick new colors. Last week, she took us to a giant paint store. There were many colors of paint there. We went by car. Pete and I chose yellow. Now our room is bright like sunshine.

State your topic, or what the story is about.

Use a voice that makes sense for your readers.

Choose words that are colorful and interesting.

1. Which sentence tells what the story is about? Underline it.

2. Circle two colorful words in the story.

3. Put a box around the sentence that sounds like it is in the wrong place.

Writer's Grammar
A noun names a person, place, or thing. Find the nouns in the Student Model.

© Harcourt

Name _____

Evaluate a Personal Story

When you evaluate a personal story, ask yourself:

- Does the writer state the topic of the story?
- Does the writer make sense?
- Does the writer use colorful words?

A. Reread the Student Model on page 47. Then answer the questions.

1. What colorful word does the writer use to describe the paint store?

   _____

2. What colorful words does the writer use to tell about the new color of his room?

   _____

B. Now evaluate the Student Model. Put a check in the box next to each thing the writer has done well. If you do not think the writer did a good job with something, do not check the box.

☐ The writer stated the topic of the story.
☐ The writer told what happened.
☐ The writer made sense.
☐ The writer used colorful words whenever he could.

C. How do you think the writer could improve the story to make it more interesting?

_____

_____

_____

See the rubric on page 207 for another way to evaluate the Student Model.

© Harcourt

Name _____

Revise by Adding Colorful Words

One thing the writer could have done better is to use more colorful words. Here is an example of how a sentence from the Student Model can be improved.

Example Pete and I wanted to repaint our room.

Pete and I were dying to repaint our boring room.

A. Revise these sentences from the Student Model. Add colorful words from the Word Bank.

1. There were many colors of paint there.

   _____

   _____

2. It was plain and white.

   _____

   _____

3. Pete and I chose yellow.

   _____

   _____

Word Bank

cheery
colorless
fun
kind of dull
rows
_____
_____
_____
_____

B. Revise the sentences you wrote on page 46. Try adding another colorful word to each sentence.

_____

_____

_____

_____

© Harcourt

49

Name _____

Look at See, Hear, Smell, Touch, and Taste Words

Some colorful words describe what we see, hear, smell, touch, or taste. These words add detail to a story.

A. Read the following model. Find the colorful words in the sentences.

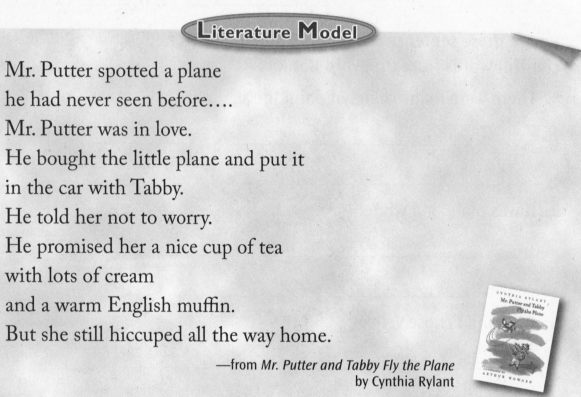

Literature Model

Mr. Putter spotted a plane
he had never seen before….
Mr. Putter was in love.
He bought the little plane and put it
in the car with Tabby.
He told her not to worry.
He promised her a nice cup of tea
with lots of cream
and a warm English muffin.
But she still hiccuped all the way home.

—from *Mr. Putter and Tabby Fly the Plane*
by Cynthia Rylant

B. Identify the colorful words.

1. Circle the colorful word in the first sentence that means Mr. Putter *saw* a plane.

2. Underline the colorful words that describe what Tabby will taste.

C. Write three colorful words that could describe how something feels.

_____

_____

© Harcourt

Name _____

Explore See, Hear, Smell, Touch, and Taste Words

You need to use your five senses for some **colorful words.** Your five senses are seeing, hearing, smelling, touching, and tasting.

See	Hear	Smell	Touch	Taste
green shadow	squeak chirp	pine lemon	soft dry	yummy sweet

A. Underline the colorful word or words in each sentence. Then circle the sense it describes.

Example The stove was <u>burning hot</u>.

(touch)   taste

1. The lemons were very sour.

   smell   taste

2. The striped ball rolled down the hill.

   touch   see

3. The baby chick chirped loudly.

   hear   touch

B. Read these sentences from *Mr. Putter and Tabby Fly the Plane.* Underline the colorful words that tell about a sense. Then write the sense on the line.

Mr. Putter cheered. Tabby purred and hiccupped.

_____

C. Suppose you are at the grocery store. Write some colorful words about a fruit or a vegetable.

_____

_____

Name _____

Use See, Hear, Smell, Touch, and Taste Words

Some colorful words use a reader's sense of seeing, hearing, or touching. Here's how one student used these three senses to write about his favorite toy.

Example

My Favorite Toy: _My Bike_

See	Hear	Touch
two wheels red gears	loud honk	squeeze bump

A. Think about your favorite toy. Write its name on the line. Then fill out the chart.

My Favorite Toy: _____

See	Hear	Touch

B. Use the information from your chart to help you write three sentences about your favorite toy. Finish on another sheet of paper.

_____

_____

_____

_____

Name _____

The Parts of a Paragraph that Describes

Paragraphs that describe give details to make a story interesting. Colorful words in paragraphs help readers form pictures in their minds.

Student Model

DRAFT

My Favorite Toy
by Alex

My favorite toy is my bike. My bike has two wheels. My bike is bright red. It has a seat and handlebars. My bike has a horn. When I squeeze it, it makes a loud honk. I don't like riding up a hill. Riding uphill makes me tired. I like to bump over the curb. I like to ride downhill. I love my bike.

> The **topic sentence** tells what the paragraph will be about.

> Colorful words **describe** and add details about the writer's bike.

1. Underline the topic sentence.

2. Circle a word or words that help you *see* what the bike looks like.

3. Draw a box around a word or words that help you *hear* what the bike sounds like.

Writer's Grammar
Adjectives are words that describe something. In the sentence "My dog is brown and fluffy," the words *brown* and *fluffy* are adjectives. Look for adjectives in the paragraph.

Writer's Companion ▪ UNIT 2
Lesson 3 *See, Hear, Smell, Touch, and Taste Words*

Name _____

Evaluate a Paragraph that Describes

When you evaluate a paragraph that describes, ask yourself:

- Does the paragraph have a topic sentence?
- Does the paragraph include detail sentences?
- Does the writer use colorful words?

A. Reread the Student Model on page 53. Then answer these questions.

1. Where is the topic sentence in the paragraph?

_____

2. What colorful word does the writer use to describe the feel of riding over the curb?

_____

B. Now evaluate the Student Model. Put a check in the box next to each thing the writer has done well. If you do not think the writer did a good job with something, do not check the box.

☐ The paragraph has a topic sentence.
☐ The detail sentences describe what the bike looks, feels, and sounds like.
☐ The writer used colorful words wherever possible.

C. How do you think the writer could improve the story?

_____

_____

_____

See the rubric on page 207 for another
way to evaluate the Student Model.

© Harcourt

Name _____

Revise by Adding Colorful Words

One thing the writer could have done better is to use more colorful words to describe the bike. Here is an example of how to revise a sentence from the Student Model.

Example My bike has a horn

My bike has a big horn.

A. **Revise these sentences from the Student Model. Use colorful words to add detail. Find words in the Word Bank.**

1. It has a seat and handlebars.

_____

_____

2. I like to ride downhill.

_____

_____

3. I don't like riding up a hill.

_____

_____

Word Bank

black
fast
silver
steep
_____
_____
_____
_____
_____

B. **Revise the sentences you wrote on page 52. Try adding another colorful word to each sentence. Finish on another sheet of paper.**

_____

_____

_____

_____

© Harcourt

Writer's Companion • UNIT 2
Lesson 3 *See, Hear, Smell, Touch,
and Taste Words*

Name _____

Review Voice and Word Choice

Writers use dialogue to show that a character is talking. They use colorful words to make a story seem alive. They choose words that make you see, hear, smell, touch, and taste.

A. Read the sentences below.

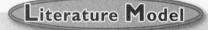

"You can butter the pan," said Hedgehog. Owl was happy. She stuck her wing into the butter. Then she smeared it around the pan.

Owl turned on the oven with her buttery feathers. She turned it up as high as it would go.

"The oven must be nice and hot," she said.

—from *Hedgehog Bakes a Cake*
by Maryann Macdonald

B. Review colorful words and dialogue.

  1. Circle a word that tells about touch.

  2. Underline a colorful word.

C. How does a writer show dialogue in the story?

_____

_____

© Harcourt

Name _____

Review Voice and Word Choice

Good writers choose words carefully to make their story fun and interesting. Colorful words can describe things you can see, hear, smell, touch, and taste.

See	Hear	Smell	Touch	Taste
yellow	swish	lemony	squish	sweet

A. Read the sentences from *Doggone Lemonade Stand*. Then answer the questions.

> Finally, all the lemon quarters were squished, squashed, or squirted. Christopher tossed some sugar into the pitcher, stirred and sloshed, and headed out the door.
>
> There was Doofus, the neighborhood dog.
>
> "My lemonade won't be safe until that dog is gone," said Christopher.

B. Write each answer on the line.

1. Which colorful words describe the lemon quarters?

_____

2. Which colorful words describe what Christopher did with the sugar?

_____

3. Underline the dialogue.

C. Pretend that you have a lemonade stand. What would you say to a customer about your lemonade? Write your words in dialogue.

_____

_____

_____

© Harcourt

Name _____

Review Voice and Word Choice

Before you write a story, think of where it takes place and who
the characters will be. Write colorful words about the characters
and the setting. Write a line of dialogue that a character might
say in the story. Here is how one child planned a story.

Example **Title:** *The Baby Princess and the Pea*

The setting: Castle, big, with pointy towers

Characters: a crying baby princess, a queen, a king, and a hard,
green pea

Dialogue: "Just like her mother," said the king.

A. Think about the plans for the story above. Answer questions about
dialogue and word choice.

1. Who is speaking in the dialogue?

_____

2. If you touched the pea, how would it feel?

_____

3. Which colorful words are used to describe the princess?

_____

B. Think about something the queen might say to the princess. Write the
queen's dialogue on the lines.

_____

_____

_____

_____

Name _____

The Parts of a Story

A good **story** introduces the characters and tells about the *setting,* or where the story is happening. A story must also have a beginning, middle, and end.

Student Model

The Baby Princess and the Pea
by Jessie

DRAFT

Once upon a time there was a big castle with pointy towers. In it lived a queen, a king, and a baby princess. They were not happy. The baby princess cried and screamed. This went on every night. When the queen picked the princess up, her crying stopped. When she put her in her crib, she screamed. "What should we do?" said the queen. The king had an idea. He lifted up the mattress. Under the mattress was a hard, little, green pea. "Just like her mother," said the king.

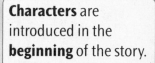

> **Characters** are introduced in the **beginning** of the story.

> The **setting** tells about the place the story happens.

> **Events** are what happen in the story. All stories have a beginning, middle, and end.

> At the **end,** the writer shows how the character solves the problem.

1. Underline the sentence that introduces the characters.
2. Circle the words that tell what the castle looks like.
3. Put a box around the sentence that states the problem.

Writer's Grammar
The word *cry* is a verb. It tells something that is happening. Look for different forms of *cry* in the story.

Name _____

Evaluate a Story

A. Two students rewrote their favorite tales. The writing below got a score of 4. A score of 4 means excellent. As you read, think about the teacher's notes.

Student Model

DRAFT

Day and Night
by Sam

Once upon a time, there was a tricky Raven. He stole the sun and put it in a box for a long time. The world was dark. There was no day. There was only night. People were sad. Then the Raven opened the box and let out the sun. Now the world was bright! People were excited. Plants grew tall. Fish swam in the rivers. Birds flew in the sky. The sun was out for many days. People could not sleep. It was hot all the time. "Raven," they said, "It's too sunny!" Raven said, "I will put the sun back in the box every day. Then it will be dark." The people cheered. They were happy. Now they had the sun to play in. Then they could sleep in the dark.

> Good job! You introduce the main character at the **beginning** of the story.

> You use colorful words to tell how people feel.

> You included dialogue in the **middle** of your story.

> Nice **ending** to your story. Good work!

© Harcourt

Name _____

B. This paragraph got a score of 2. Why did it get a low score?

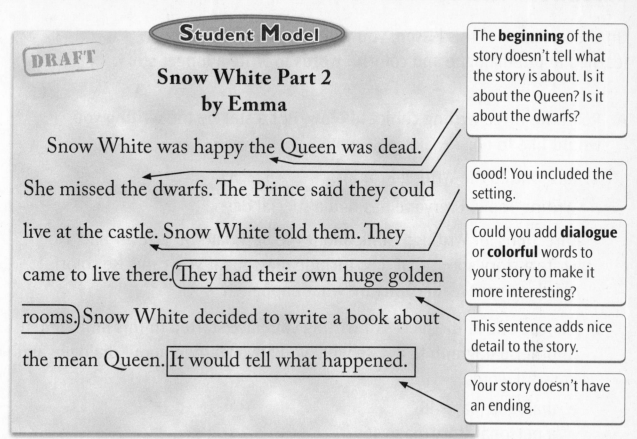

Student Model

DRAFT

Snow White Part 2
by Emma

Snow White was happy the Queen was dead. She missed the dwarfs. The Prince said they could live at the castle. Snow White told them. They came to live there. They had their own huge golden rooms. Snow White decided to write a book about the mean Queen. It would tell what happened.

The **beginning** of the story doesn't tell what the story is about. Is it about the Queen? Is it about the dwarfs?

Good! You included the setting.

Could you add **dialogue** or **colorful** words to your story to make it more interesting?

This sentence adds nice detail to the story.

Your story doesn't have an ending.

C. What score would you give the student's story? Put a number on each line.

	4	3	2	1
Word Choice _____	☐ The writer used colorful words in the story.	☐ The writer used some colorful words in the story.	☐ The writer needs more colorful words in the story.	☐ The writer does not use colorful words in the story.
Voice _____	☐ The writer's voice is very clear.	☐ The writer's voice is clear.	☐ The writer's voice is not very clear.	☐ The writer's voice is not clear at all.
Sentences _____	☐ The writer used dialogue and quotation marks correctly.	☐ The writer used dialogue and quotation marks correctly most of the time.	☐ A bit of the dialogue is incorrect.	☐ The writer did not use dialogue at all.

© Harcourt

Name _____

Extended Writing/Test Prep

On the last page of this lesson, you will use what you have
learned about dialogue and colorful words to write a longer story.

A. Read the three writing choices below. Put a star by the writing you
would like to do.

1. Respond to the Writing Prompt.

Writing Topic: Everyone has had a special day.

Directions for Writing: Think about the best day you've ever had. Now
write a story about that day. Include dialogue if you can. Use colorful
words to help readers picture what happened.

2. Choose one of the pieces of writing you have started in this unit. Add
another paragraph to it. Use what you have learned about dialogue and
colorful words.

- dialogue (page 40)
- a personal story (page 46)
- a paragraph that describes (page 52)

3. Choose a new topic and write a new story. Use colorful words to help
the reader picture what you are writing about.

B. Use the space below to plan your writing.

TITLE: _____

OPENING OR TOPIC SENTENCE: _____

_____

_____

© Harcourt

Name _____

C. In the space below, draw a chart that will help you plan your writing. Fill in the chart.

Notes

_____

_____

_____

_____

_____

_____

_____

_____

D. Now do your writing on another sheet of paper.

Writer's Companion • UNIT 2
Lesson 4 *Review Voice and Word Choice*

Name _____

Answering Multiple-Choice Questions

Some writing tests have questions with answer choices. This lesson will help you practice this kind of test.

A. Read the test tip. Then answer the questions.

Answer questions 1–4 on the Answer Sheet.

1. Which sentence is written correctly?

   A   My friend Rachel went to Chicago last week.

   B   My friend Rachel went to chicago last week.

   C   My Friend Rachel went to Chicago last week.

2. Which sentence is written correctly?

   F   Tracy and mike live near Baker field

   G   Tracy and Mike live near baker Field.

   H   Tracy and Mike live near Baker Field.

3. Which sentence is written correctly?

   A   Foxes are very fast-running animals.

   B   Foxs are very fast-running animales.

   C   Foxes are very fast. Running animals.

4. Which sentence is written correctly?

   F   There are five cow over in that field.

   G   There are five cows over in that field.

   H   There are five cows over in that fields.

Test Tip:

A noun names a person, place or thing. A proper noun names a particular person, place or thing. Proper nouns begin with capital letters.

© Harcourt

Answer all test questions on this Answer Sheet.	
1. Ⓐ Ⓑ Ⓒ	3. Ⓐ Ⓑ Ⓒ
2. Ⓕ Ⓖ Ⓗ	4. Ⓕ Ⓖ Ⓗ

Name _____

B. **Read the test tip. Then read the passage that follows.**
Read each question and fill in the correct answer.

(1) My trip to Maine was very exciting. (2) We visited my cousin's farm. (3) There were several sheep and horses near the barn. (4) In the woods were two huge mooses. (5) There also were deer and raccoons. (6) We watched a beaver chew a tree with its big tooths. (7) We all said our trip to Maine was the best ever!

Answer questions 1–3 on the Answer Sheet.

1. What change, if any, should be made to sentence 3?

   A Change *sheep* to **sheep's**

   B Change *sheep* to **sheeps**

   C Change *several* to **severals**

   D Make no change

> **Test Tip:**
> Some nouns do not become plural by adding –s or –es. Examples of nouns that become plural in different ways are *goose→geese* and *deer → deer.*

2. What change, if any, should be made to sentence 4?

   F Change *woods* to **wood**

   G Change *were* to **was**

   H Change *mooses* to **moose**

   J Make no change

3. What change, if any, should be made to sentence 6?

   A Change *beaver* to **beaver**

   B Change *tree* to **trees**

   C Change *tooth* to **teeth**

   D Make no change

© Harcourt

Answer all test questions on this Answer Sheet.

1. Ⓐ Ⓑ Ⓒ Ⓓ   3. Ⓐ Ⓑ Ⓒ Ⓓ

2. Ⓕ Ⓖ Ⓗ Ⓙ

Name _____

C. Read the test tip. Then answer the questions.

Read each question. Then mark the circle next to the correct answer.

1. Which sentence is written correctly?
   Ⓐ anna ran to the park.
   Ⓑ Anna ran to the park.
   Ⓒ Anna Ran to the park.
   Ⓓ Anna ran to The Park.

Test Tip:
Think about words that need capital letters as you read these questions.

2. Which sentence is written correctly?
   Ⓐ Miranda and Elizabeth read a book together.
   Ⓑ Miranda and Elizabeth read a Book together.
   Ⓒ Miranda and elizabeth read a book together.
   Ⓓ Miranda and Elizabeth Read a Book Together.

3. Which of these is a complete sentence?
   Ⓐ The person next to me.
   Ⓑ Ayesha and all our friends.
   Ⓒ Dad fixed a big salad.
   Ⓓ Went on a class picnic.

4. Which of these is a complete sentence?
   Ⓐ My best friend Tonya and her grandmother.
   Ⓑ Always soccer together on Saturday.
   Ⓒ Went to the movies last night.
   Ⓓ Dan and I raced home.

D. Read the test tip. Then answer the questions.

Read the paragraph. Then read each question. Mark
the correct answer on the Answer Sheet.

(1) We are studying sound with mrs. ward. (2) We banged
on drums in blair park. (3) I could feel the sound waves in my
chest. (4) The gooses in the park flew away. (5) All those drums
were loud!

1. What is the **BEST** way to fix sentence 1?

A We are studying sound with mrs. ward.

B We are studying sound with Mrs. Ward.

C We are studying sound with Mrs. ward.

D Make no change

2. What is the **BEST** way to fix sentence 2?

F We Banged on drums in blair park.

G We banged on drums in blair Park.

H We banged on drums in Blair Park.

J Make no change

3. What is the **BEST** way to fix sentence 4?

A The geeses in the park flew away.

B The gooses in the park flew away.

C The geese in the park flew away.

D Make no change

> **Test Tip:**
> Be sure to
> read the whole
> paragraph first.
> Always reread
> the numbered
> sentences before
> you choose your
> answer.

© Harcourt

Answer all test questions on this Answer Sheet.

1. Ⓐ Ⓑ Ⓒ Ⓓ   3. Ⓐ Ⓑ Ⓒ Ⓓ

2. Ⓕ Ⓖ Ⓗ Ⓙ

Name _____

Look at Facts and Reasons

A **topic sentence** tells the main idea of a paragraph. The other sentences give **details** about the topic. They tell **facts and reasons**.

A. Read these lines from Johnny Appleseed. Look for the topic sentence and the detail sentences.

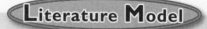

Narrator: When Johnny was a boy, many of his neighbors were moving out west. They were pioneers on the wild frontier. Johnny decided that when he became a man, he would also go out west. He wanted to plant apple seeds everywhere he went. That way, the pioneers would have apples to eat at their new homes.

—from *Johnny Appleseed*
by Pleasant DeSpain

B. Find the topic sentence and detail sentences.
   1. Put a box around the topic sentence.
   2. Underline a detail sentence.

C. Why did Johnny Appleseed go out west? Write a reason on the lines.

_____

_____

_____

Name _____

Explore Facts and Reasons

A topic sentence tells you the main idea of a paragraph. Detail sentences give facts and reasons.

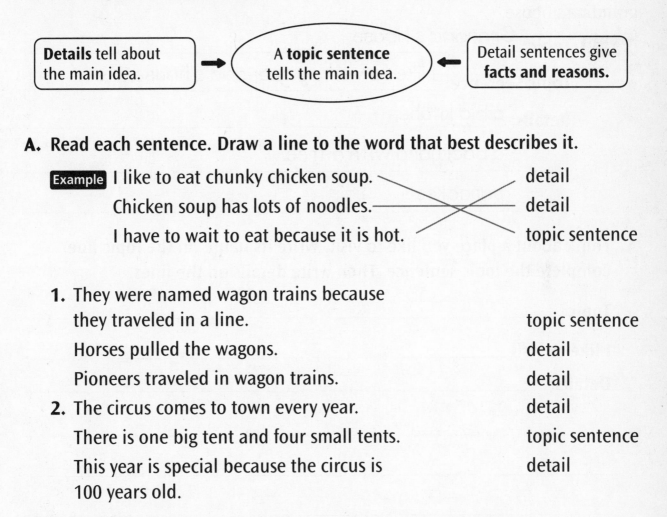

| Details tell about the main idea. | → | A topic sentence tells the main idea. | ← | Detail sentences give facts and reasons. |

A. Read each sentence. Draw a line to the word that best describes it.

Example I like to eat chunky chicken soup. — detail

Chicken soup has lots of noodles. — detail

I have to wait to eat because it is hot. — topic sentence

1. They were named wagon trains because they traveled in a line.   topic sentence

Horses pulled the wagons.   detail

Pioneers traveled in wagon trains.   detail

2. The circus comes to town every year.   detail

There is one big tent and four small tents.   topic sentence

This year is special because the circus is 100 years old.   detail

B. Read these lines. Underline the facts and circle the reason.

Narrator: Johnny left home at age 23.

Chorus: He walked and walked and he planted and planted.

Narrator: 'Cause he had itchy feet!

C. Imagine that you have itchy feet, too. Write a sentence about why your feet are itchy. If you need more space, use another sheet of paper.

_____

_____

© Harcourt

Name _____

Use Facts and Reasons

Before you write, think of a topic. Write a topic sentence. Then write down some details. Here's what a student wrote about her grandma's house.

Example **Topic:** _Grandma's House_

Topic Sentence: _I like to visit my grandma's house._

Details: _a big kitchen_

a backyard with a tree

pancakes

A. Think about a place you like to visit. Write its name on the topic line. Complete the topic sentence. Then write details on the lines.

Topic: _____

I like to visit _____.

Details: _____

_____

_____

_____

B. Now, write three sentences about the place you like to visit.

_____

_____

_____

_____

_____

© Harcourt

Name _____

The Parts of a Paragraph That Gives Information

A good **paragraph** starts with a topic sentence. Here is a paragraph written by a second grader. As you read, think about how the student uses details. Then answer the questions.

Student Model

DRAFT

Visiting Grandma
by Sarah

I like to visit my grandma. I love her big, warm kitchen because there are always yummy pancakes to eat. I like to play with her dog. I have lots of fun playing in her backyard. I really like the tree.

A topic sentence tells the main idea.

Detail sentences give facts and reasons and tell about the main idea.

1. Which is the topic sentence? Put a box around it.
2. Which are detail sentences? Underline them.
3. Draw a wavy line under a reason.
4. Why else does Sarah like to visit her grandma? Write a reason on the lines.

_____

_____

_____

_____

Writer's Grammar
The first word of each sentence starts with a capital letter. All sentences have an end mark. Find the capital letters in the paragraph above.

Writer's Companion • UNIT 3
Lesson 1 *Facts and Reasons*

Name _____

Evaluate a Paragraph That Gives Information

When you evaluate a paragraph that gives information, ask
yourself these questions:

- Does the writer tell you the main idea?

- Does the writer give you facts and reasons?

A. Use the Student Model on page 71 to answer these questions.

   1. What is the main idea of the paragraph?

   _____

   2. Why does the writer like her grandma's kitchen?

   _____

   _____

B. Now evaluate the Student Model. Check each thing the writer did well.

   ☐ The topic sentence states the main idea.
   ☐ The writer gave facts.
   ☐ The writer gave reasons.

C. How could the writer make the paragraph better? Write your ideas.

_____

_____

_____

_____

© Harcourt

See the rubric on page 207 for another
way to evaluate the Student Model.

Name _____

Revise by Adding Facts and Reasons

One thing the writer could have done better is to give more facts and reasons. Here is one way to make a sentence in the Student Model better.

Example I like to play with her dog.

I like to play with her dog because he likes to fetch.

_____

A. Revise these sentences from the Student Model. Add facts and reasons. Use the Word Bank to help you.

Word Bank
big
grassy
hiding place
old
oak
special
trunk

1. I have lots of fun playing in her backyard.

_____

_____

2. I really like the tree.

_____

_____

B. Revise the sentences you wrote on page 70. Add facts and reasons.

_____

_____

_____

_____

_____

_____

_____

Writer's Companion ▪ UNIT 3
Lesson 1 *Facts and Reasons*

Name _____

Look at Staying Focused

All **ideas** in a paragraph must tell about the **topic sentence**.

A. Read the following model. Look for the topic sentence and the ideas.

Literature Model

The wind scatters seeds. Some seeds have fluff on them that lets them float to the ground like tiny parachutes. Others have wings that spin as they fall.

—from *From Seed to Plant*
by Gail Gibbons

B. Identify the topic sentence and ideas.
1. Underline the topic sentence.
2. Circle two ideas that tell about the topic.

C. What helps seeds spin?

_____

Name _____

Explore Staying Focused

Detail sentences tell facts about the topic sentence
in a paragraph.

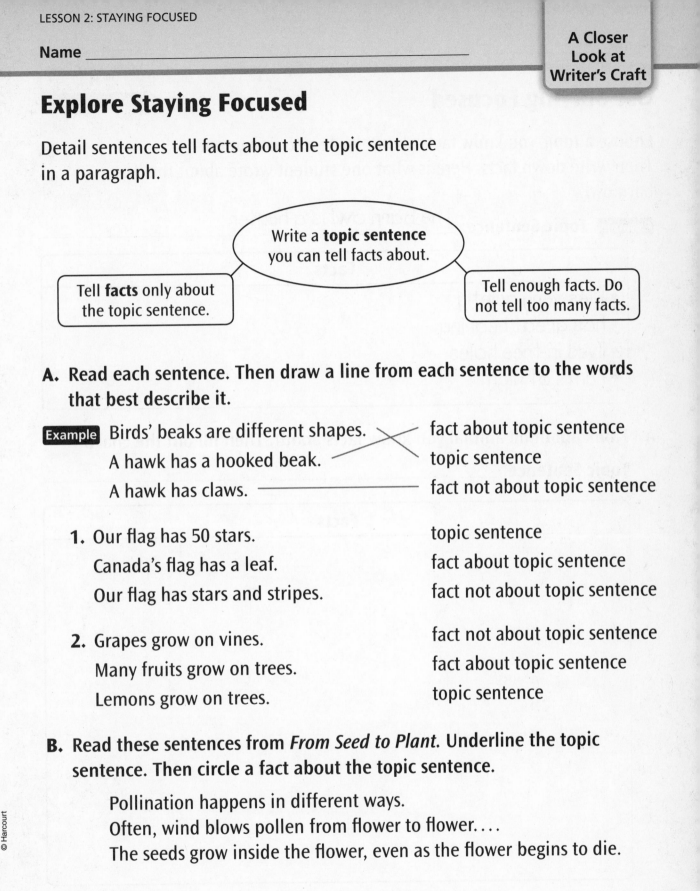

Write a **topic sentence**
you can tell facts about.

Tell **facts** only about
the topic sentence.

Tell enough facts. Do
not tell too many facts.

A. Read each sentence. Then draw a line from each sentence to the words
that best describe it.

Example   Birds' beaks are different shapes.   fact about topic sentence

A hawk has a hooked beak.   topic sentence

A hawk has claws.   fact not about topic sentence

1. Our flag has 50 stars.   topic sentence

Canada's flag has a leaf.   fact about topic sentence

Our flag has stars and stripes.   fact not about topic sentence

2. Grapes grow on vines.   fact not about topic sentence

Many fruits grow on trees.   fact about topic sentence

Lemons grow on trees.   topic sentence

B. Read these sentences from *From Seed to Plant*. Underline the topic
sentence. Then circle a fact about the topic sentence.

Pollination happens in different ways.
Often, wind blows pollen from flower to flower....
The seeds grow inside the flower, even as the flower begins to die.

Name _____

Use Staying Focused

Choose a topic you know facts about. Write a topic sentence. Then write down facts. Here is what one student wrote about the barn owl.

Example **Topic Sentence:** ___The barn owl is a hunter.___

Facts
• flies very quietly • has great hearing • lives in tree holes • hunts at night

A. Think about an animal you know facts about. Then fill out the chart.

Topic Sentence: _____

Facts

B. Write three sentences about your topic. Use your facts. Use another sheet of paper.

© Harcourt

Name _____

The Parts of a Paragraph That Gives Information

A **paragraph that gives information** includes a topic sentence and facts about the topic sentence. Here is a draft written by a second grader. As you read, think about how the student uses facts. Then answer the questions.

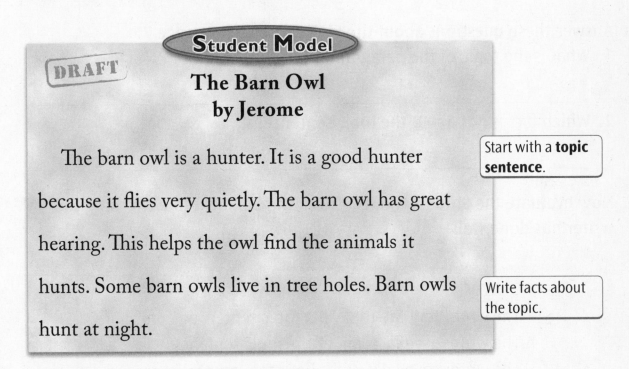

Student Model

DRAFT

The Barn Owl
by Jerome

The barn owl is a hunter. It is a good hunter because it flies very quietly. The barn owl has great hearing. This helps the owl find the animals it hunts. Some barn owls live in tree holes. Barn owls hunt at night.

Start with a **topic sentence**.

Write facts about the topic.

1. Which is the topic sentence? Circle it.
2. Which sentences tell facts about the topic sentence? Underline them.

© Harcourt

Writer's Grammar
A pronoun is a word that takes the place of a noun. *I*, *it*, and *you* are pronouns. Look for pronouns in the Student Model.

Name _____

Evaluate a Paragraph That Gives Information

When you study a paragraph that gives information, ask yourself these questions:

- Does the writer tell you the topic of the paragraph?
- Does the writer give you facts only about the topic sentence?

A. Answer these questions about the Student Model on page 77.
  1. What is the topic of the paragraph?

  _____

  2. Which fact is **not** about the topic sentence?

  _____

B. Now evaluate the Student Model. Check the box next to each thing the writer has done well.

  ☐ The writer told the topic in a topic sentence.
  ☐ The writer gave facts about the topic sentence.
  ☐ The writer gave facts only about the topic sentence.

C. How do you think the writer could make the paragraph better? Write your ideas below.

  _____

  _____

  _____

© Harcourt

See the rubric on page 207 for another way to evaluate the Student Model.

Name _____

Revise by Taking Out and Adding Facts

The writer could have taken out the fact that is not about the topic sentence. Then the writer could give more information about the topic. Here is one way to revise the Student Model.

Example **Take out:** Some barn owls live in tree holes.

Add fact: _Barn owls hunt to feed their hungry babies._

A. Revise the Student Model by adding facts about the barn owl's hunting. Use the Word Bank for ideas.

Word Bank
dark
hunt
mice
see
well
_____
_____

1. _____

_____

2. _____

_____

B. Revise your writing on page 76. Take out any fact that is not about your topic sentence. Add a sentence with a fact about your topic. Use another sheet of paper if you need to.

_____

_____

_____

_____

_____

_____

_____

_____

Writer's Companion • UNIT 3
Lesson 2 _Staying Focused_

Name _____

Look at Putting Your Ideas Together

Sometimes a writer gathers **facts** about a topic from different books and magazines. Look in books or on the Internet. The writer takes notes and uses the notes to tell about a topic.

A. Read the following model. Look for a fact. Then look for a reason that explains the fact.

Literature Model

In the cold chill of winter, most broad-leaved trees have no leaves. The leaves have dropped off because there is less sunlight.

—from *The Secret Life of Trees*
by Chiara Chevallier

B. Find a fact and reason about the topic.
   1. What is the topic? Circle it.
   2. Underline a sentence that gives a fact and a reason.

C. Why have the leaves dropped off? Write your answer on the lines.

_____

_____

© Harcourt

Name _____

Explore Putting Your Ideas Together

When you write, each paragraph needs a topic sentence and detail sentences.

The **topic sentence** of each paragraph tells the main idea.

Some writing has **two paragraphs**.

Detail sentences give facts and reasons about each main idea.

A. Put a box around the topic sentence. Underline the detail sentence that gives a fact and a reason.

Example | A compass is a tool. | It has a needle. A compass helps you find directions because the needle always points north.

1. A magnet can pull some objects. It can pull objects made of iron. A magnet can pull a nail because a nail is made of iron.

2. The cactus is a kind of plant. It is a desert plant. A cactus needs little water, so it can live in the desert.

B. Read these sentences from *The Secret Life of Trees*. Underline the detail sentence that tells where the seed is.

This palm tree's seed is inside its hairy coconut shell. The shell contains milk so the seed can start growing even if it is washed up somewhere dry.

C. Write a detail sentence about watermelon seeds.

_____

_____

© Harcourt

Name _____

Use Putting Your Ideas Together

Think of a topic you want to learn about. Find detailed information about your topic. Here is what one student wrote about fish.

Example

Topic: Fish
Facts and Reasons
have scales have gills so they can breathe in water have fins to move in water pufferfish is one kind of fish puffs up body to scare enemies

A. Choose a topic you want to learn about. Fill in the chart.

Topic:
Facts and Reasons

© Harcourt

B. Now write a paragraph about your topic. Be sure you have a topic sentence and detail sentences. Use another sheet of paper.

Name _____

The Parts of a Research Report

A **research report** gives facts about a topic. It has a title, a main topic, and facts and reasons that tell about the main topic.

Student Model

DRAFT

Fish
by Monica

A fish is one kind of animal. Fish have gills, fins, and scales. They have gills so they can breathe in water. Other animals use lungs to breathe. Fish can move in the water because they have fins.

Fish protect themselves in different ways. A pufferfish lives in the ocean. A pufferfish is a fish that can puff up its body. Then it looks big! The reason it puffs up is to scare away its enemies.

> The title tells the **topic** of the research report.

> The research report has a sentence that tells the **main topic**.

> Detail sentences give **facts** and **reasons** about the main topic.

1. How do you think the pufferfish got its name?

   _____

2. Why does the pufferfish puff up?

   _____

© Harcourt

Writer's Grammar
Commas are used between three or more words in a series. Look for a series with commas in the Student Model.

Name _____

Evaluate a Research Report

When you study a research report, ask yourself these questions:

- Does the writer tell you what the research report is mostly about?
- Does the writer tell you what each paragraph is about?
- Does the writer give facts and reasons about the topic?

A. Reread the Student Model on page 83. Then answer these questions.

   1. What is the research report mostly about?

   _____

   2. What is the first paragraph about?

   _____

   3. Why can fish move in water?

   _____

B. Now evaluate the Student Model. Put a check in the box next to each thing the writer has done well. If you do not think the writer did a good job with something, do not check the box.

   ☐ Each topic sentence tells what the paragraph is about.
   ☐ The writer gave facts and reasons tied closely to the topic.

C. How do you think the writer could make the research report better?

_____

_____

See the rubric on page 207 for another way to evaluate the Student Model.

© Harcourt

Name _____

Revise a Research Report

The student writer could have made sure that all detail sentences give facts about the topic sentence. Here is an example of taking out a fact not tied to the topic sentence and adding a new fact.

Example **Take out:** _Other animals use lungs to breathe._

Add: _Scales cover the bodies of fish._

A. Revise the second paragraph of the Student Model by taking out any fact not tied to the topic sentence. Add a fact about the topic. Use the Word Bank for ideas.

Word Bank

protect

pufferfish

some

spines

_____

_____

1. Take out: _____

_____

2. Add: _____

_____

B. Revise your paragraph on page 82. Take out any fact not tied to a topic sentence. Add another fact about the topic. If you need more space, use another sheet of paper.

_____

_____

_____

_____

_____

_____

_____

© Harcourt

Name _____

Review: Organization

Writers tell the main idea in a topic sentence of a paragraph. They give detail sentences about the topic. Detail sentences tell facts and reasons.

A. Read the following model. Look for facts and reasons.

Literature Model

Jesse waited. She waited until the days were so hot she had to wear shoes so her feet wouldn't blister in the sand. So hot the air wrinkled up like an unironed shirt. So hot that hardly anything moved except the flies.

—from *Watermelon Day*
by Kathi Appelt

B. Identify the fact and the reason.
1. What is a fact about the days? Circle the fact.
2. What is the reason Jesse had to wear shoes? Underline the reason.

C. Did everything move on the hot days? Explain.

_____

_____

Name _____

Review: Organization

Writers tell facts and reasons that are about the topic sentence.

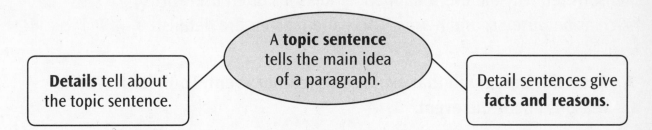

Details tell about the topic sentence.

A **topic sentence** tells the main idea of a paragraph.

Detail sentences give **facts and reasons**.

A. Read the paragraph. Look for facts and reasons about the topic sentence.

> Many spiders build webs to catch insects. Some webs are made up of sticky threads. Insects stick to the threads in the web. The spider does not stick to the threads because it has oil on its body. A spider has eight legs.

B. Find parts of the paragraph.
1. Circle the topic sentence.
2. Underline a detail about the topic sentence.
3. Put a box around a sentence that is not tied to the topic.

C. Read this paragraph from *Watermelon Day*. Underline the topic sentence. Circle a fact about it.

> Jesse's watermelon floated all that hot day long. Willow branches dipped up and down, testing the icy water. That melon floated while the cousins came.

© Harcourt

87

Name _____

Review: Organization

When writers tell about an event, they give facts and reasons.
Reasons tell why the event happened. Reasons often use words
such as *because, so,* and *reason.* Facts and reasons are details.

A. Read this paragraph that explains a weather event. Look for facts and
reasons about the event.

> Rain comes from clouds. Clouds have different shapes.
> Clouds form because there is water in the air. Sometimes
> clouds get too full of water. The reason is that the air is cooled.
> Water falls from the clouds because they can't hold the water
> any longer.

B. Answer the questions.
   1. Why do clouds form?

   _____

   2. Why does water fall from the clouds?

   _____

C. Which fact is NOT about the topic? Circle the fact.

© Harcourt

Name _____

The Parts of a Paragraph of Explanation

A **paragraph that explains** should tell about an event, or what happened, in the topic sentence. Detail sentences should tell reasons why the event happened.

A. Below is a draft written by a second grader. As you read, think about what happens, and why it happens. Then answer the questions.

DRAFT

How a Tornado Forms
by Beth

A tornado begins on a hot day. First a big cloud forms because cold air comes in. The cold air crashes into the hot air and causes spinning winds in the cloud. Then a tornado twists out of the big cloud. This is the reason a tornado is also called a twister.

> A **topic sentence** tells the event.

> A **detail sentence** tells what happens and why.

> Other **detail sentences** tell what happens and why.

1. What does the paragraph explain?

_____

2. What makes the wind spin in the big cloud?

_____

_____

3. Underline the topic sentence.

Writer's Grammar
When you write a paragraph that explains, use words such as *because, so, reason,* and *causes.* Find examples of three of those words in the student model.

Name _____

Evaluate a Paragraph of Explanation

A. Two students wrote a paragraph that explains a weather event. The paragraph below got a score of 4. A score of 4 means excellent. As you read, think about the teacher's notes.

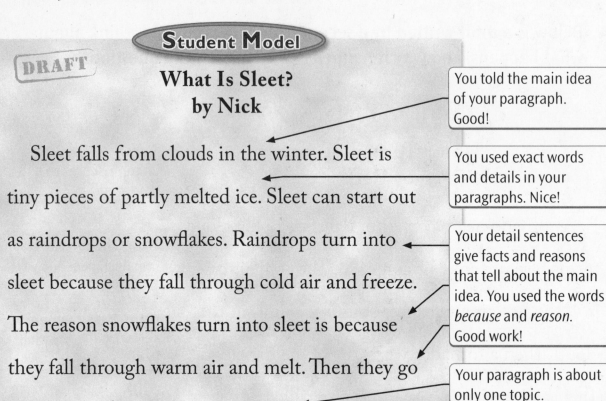

Student Model

DRAFT

What Is Sleet?
by Nick

Sleet falls from clouds in the winter. Sleet is tiny pieces of partly melted ice. Sleet can start out as raindrops or snowflakes. Raindrops turn into sleet because they fall through cold air and freeze. The reason snowflakes turn into sleet is because they fall through warm air and melt. Then they go through cold air and become sleet.

You told the main idea of your paragraph. Good!

You used exact words and details in your paragraphs. Nice!

Your detail sentences give facts and reasons that tell about the main idea. You used the words *because* and *reason*. Good work!

Your paragraph is about only one topic.

© Harcourt

Name _____

Evaluating the Student Model

B. This paragraph got a score of 2. Why did it get a low score?

Student Model

DRAFT

Hurricanes
by Marta

A hurricane is a storm of strong wind and heavy rain. Storm clouds come together over an ocean. A hurricane forms because winds spin the clouds into a big circle. The hurricane grows for days. A blizzard is a storm of wind too. It has snow instead of rain.

> This sentence tells the main idea of a paragraph about hurricanes. You used exact words here. Good work.

> This is a good detail sentence. You tell what happens and why.

> The word *spin* is an exact word. Nice! What exact word could you use instead of *big* to describe the circle of clouds?

> Could you add a detail to tell the reason the hurricane grows? Try to find this information.

> You need to tell about hurricanes only. These sentences are about a different topic.

C. What score would you give the student's paragraph? Put a number on each line.

	4	3	2	1
Topic _____	☐ It is very clear what the paragraph is about.	☐ It is somewhat clear what the paragraph is about.	☐ It is not very clear what the paragraph is about.	☐ It is unclear what the paragraph is about.
Focus/Ideas _____	☐ All the ideas are about one topic.	☐ Almost all the ideas are about one topic.	☐ Some of the ideas are about one topic.	☐ The ideas are about different topics.
Development _____	☐ There is a good topic sentence and details that are tied to it.	☐ There is a good topic sentence and some details that are tied to it.	☐ The topic sentence is good, but the details are not tied to it.	☐ The topic sentence is not clear, and the details are not tied to it.

© Harcourt

Writer's Companion • UNIT 3
Lesson 4 *Review Organization*

Name _____

Extended Writing/Test Prep

On the last two pages of this lesson, you will write a longer
work. You will use what you have learned about topic sentences
and details that are facts and reasons.

A. Read the three choices below. Put a star by the writing you
would like to do.

1. Write about the following topic.

Writing Topic: Interesting things happen in neighborhoods.

Directions for Writing: Think about something that happened in your
neighborhood. Now write a paragraph explaining what happened. Give
reasons why this event happened.

2. Choose one of the pieces of writing you started in this unit. Write more
about the topic. Make your topic sentence and details better.

3. Choose a new topic about an event. Use detail sentences to tell about
the event.

B. Use the space below to plan your writing.

TOPIC: _____

TOPIC SENTENCE: _____

_____

_____

_____

_____

© Harcourt

Name _____

C. In the space below, draw a chart that will help you plan your writing. Fill in the chart with notes you will use.

Notes

_____

_____

_____

_____

_____

_____

_____

D. Do your writing on another sheet of paper.

Name _____

Answering Multiple-Choice Questions

On some tests, you will have to decide which sentences are written correctly. This lesson will help you practice this kind of test.

A. Read the test tip. Then answer the questions. Fill in the circle next to your answer choice.

1. In which sentence is all **capitalization** correct?
   - (A) Is thanksgiving always in November?
   - (B) Is Thanksgiving always in november?
   - (C) Is Thanksgiving always in November?

2. In which sentence is all **capitalization** correct?
   - (F) Each May, we give Mom presents on Mother's Day.
   - (G) Each May, we give Mom presents on Mother's day.
   - (H) Each may, we give Mom presents on Mother's Day.

Test Tip:
To answer questions 1 and 2, remember to capitalize proper nouns that name months, days of the week, holidays, and people.

3. In which sentence is all **punctuation** correct?
   - (A) Last July, I saw fireworks on Independence Day?
   - (B) Last July, I saw fireworks on Independence Day,
   - (C) Last July, I saw fireworks on Independence Day.

4. In which sentence is all **punctuation** and **capitalization** correct?
   - (F) When is your birthday John.
   - (G) When is your Birthday, John!
   - (H) When is your birthday, John?

Name _____

B. Some tests will ask you to decide which sentences are NOT written correctly. Read the test tip. Then answer the questions. Fill in the circle next to your answer choice.

1. Which sentence is NOT written correctly?

  (A) My brother was born on Dmbr. 2, 2003.

  (B) My sister was born on Dec. 14, 2000.

  (C) I was born on Dec. 31, 2000.

Test Tip:
To answer these questions, remember that the abbreviations of most months and days have the first three letters and a period:
January–Jan.
Wednesday–Wed.

2. Which sentence is NOT written correctly?

  (F) The show will be this Wed., June 15.

  (G) The last day to buy tickets is Mo., June 13.

  (H) There will be another show on Sun., June 19.

3. Which sentence is NOT written correctly?

  (A) The book fair is Feb. 22.

  (B) Please come to my party on Septem. 17.

  (C) A new toy store opens on Aug. 10.

4. Which sentence is NOT written correctly?

  (F) Ju. 4 is Independence day.

  (G) Thanksgiving is on a Thursday.

  (H) Martin Luther King, Jr. Day is celebrated on Monday.

Name _____

C. For some questions, you will read a paragraph. The
sentences in the paragraph will be numbered. Read the
test tip and the passage. Then answer the questions on
the Answer Sheet.

Taking a Pig to a Fair

(1) Sam has a pig. (2) Sam took the pig to his towns animal
fair. (3) The judge liked Sam pig. (4) The pig was a winner! (5)
The winner's prize was a blue ribbon.

1. Which is the correct way to write sentence 2?

  A Sam took the pig to his town animals fair.

  B Sam took the pig to his town's animal fair.

  C Sam took the pig to his town animal's fair.

  D Sam took the pig to his towns animal's fair.

> **Test Tip:**
> To answer the
> questions, think
> about words that
> show belonging or
> ownership.

2. In sentence 3, which is the correct way to write
the word that shows the pig belongs to Sam?

  F Sams

  G Sam,s

  H Sam's

  I Sams'

3. Which is the correct way to write sentence 5?

  A The winner' prize was a blue ribbon.

  B The winners prize was a blue ribbon.

  C The winner prize was a blue ribbon.

  D Leave as is.

Answer all test questions on this Answer Sheet.

  1. Ⓐ Ⓑ Ⓒ Ⓓ   **3.** Ⓐ Ⓑ Ⓒ Ⓓ

  2. Ⓕ Ⓖ Ⓗ Ⓘ

© Harcourt

Name _____

D. Some test questions may ask you to decide the best way to correct sentences in a paragraph. Read the test tip and the passage. Then answer the questions on the Answer Sheet.

Play Time

(1) Our class wrote a play. (2) It was about Martin Luther King day. (3) Last Thursday and friday, we made the set. (4) Everyone helped in some way. (5) We acted out our play on Tuesday, january 2.

1. What change, if any, should be made in sentence 2?

A   Change *day* to **Day**

B   Change *Martin* to **martin**

C   Change *It* to **it**

D   Make no change

> **Test Tip:**
> Remember that proper nouns begin with capital letters.

2. What change, if any, should be made to sentence 3?

F   Change *Thursday* to **thursday**

G   Change *set* to **Set**

H   change *friday* to **Friday**

I   Make no change

3. What change, if any, should be made to sentence 5?

A   Change *Tuesday* to **tuesday**

B   Change *january* to **January**

C   Change *play* to **Play**

D   Make no change

Answer all test questions on this Answer Sheet.

1.   Ⓐ   Ⓑ   Ⓒ   Ⓓ   3.   Ⓐ   Ⓑ   Ⓒ   Ⓓ

2.   Ⓕ   Ⓖ   Ⓗ   Ⓘ

Name _____

Look at a Good Beginning

The beginning of a story is important. A good beginning tells what the story is about. A good beginning grabs the reader's attention.

A. Read the following model. Notice how the writer begins with a paragraph that makes you want to read on.

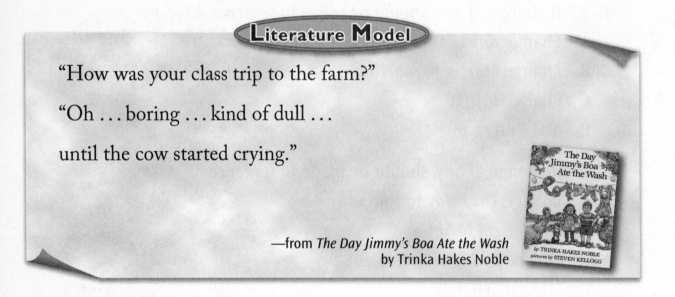

Literature Model

"How was your class trip to the farm?"

"Oh … boring … kind of dull …

until the cow started crying."

—from *The Day Jimmy's Boa Ate the Wash*
by Trinka Hakes Noble

B. Identify an interesting beginning.
   1. Underline the words that tell you what the story is about.
   2. Circle the words that really grab your attention.

C. Why do you want to read more of the story?

_____

_____

_____

Name _____

Explore a Good Beginning

Writers tell readers what the story is about.

A Good Beginning of a Story

Writers make it interesting so readers will keep reading.

A. Underline the more interesting beginning. Write what the beginning is about.

Example a. Today it was rainy. We played inside for the whole day.

   b. <u>Today it stormed. The wind howled, and the rain poured.</u>

   a rainy day _____

1. a. We got to trade lunches. I traded with Carlos.

   b. I traded for the best lunch ever last Friday!

   _____

2. a. My dog Eddie does lots of crazy tricks. He is very smart.

   b. My dog Eddie is funny. He can roll over and beg.

   _____

B. Read this story beginning about a hike. Circle the words that make you want to read on.

   We started down the steep mountain.
   Bang! There was a big clap of thunder.

C. Write another interesting sentence about the hike.

   _____

   _____

   _____

   _____

© Harcourt

Name _____

Use a Good Beginning

A good beginning is interesting and tells the reader what the story is about. Here is how one second grader began to plan a story about a trip she took.

Example What the story is about:

> trip to London, England

_____

Something interesting to begin with:

> It was the best trip of my life!

_____

A. Think about a trip you have taken, or a trip you would like to take. Fill in the lines to help you write a good beginning.
What the story is about:

_____

Something interesting to begin with:

_____

B. Use the information from above to help you write a good beginning. Then write a story about your trip. If you need more space, use another sheet of paper.

_____

_____

_____

_____

_____

_____

© Harcourt

Name _____

The Parts of a Personal Story

A **personal story** tells about something that happened to the writer. Below is a draft by a second grader. As you read, think about the parts of the story.

Student Model

DRAFT

Lila in London
by Lila

I went on the best trip of my life last summer.

My family and I went to London, England. We

took a very long plane ride over the Atlantic Ocean.

The ride was amazing! Everything on the ground

looked tiny to me. I had so much fun in London.

I went to a soccer game. Soccer is called "football"

there. I saw Big Ben and heard it chime. Last, I

took a boat ride on the Thames River. I rode on the

biggest Ferris wheel in the world. I felt like I could

see forever! I was sad to come home.

> **A good beginning** interests the reader.

> This story has **a beginning, a middle, and an ending.**

> There are **time-order** words.

> Use words like **me, my,** and **I.**

> Use **details** to describe things.

1. Underline the words in the beginning sentence that make you want to read more.
2. Draw circles around *I, me,* and *my.*
3. Put a box around a word that shows time order.

Writer's Grammar

A proper noun names a special person, place, or thing and begins with a capital letter. Find the proper nouns in the story.

© Harcourt

Name _____

Evaluate a Personal Story

When you evaluate a personal story, ask yourself:

- Does the beginning get the reader's attention?
- Does the story have a clear beginning, middle, and ending?
- Does the story include time-order words?
- Does the writer use *I, me,* and *my*?

A. Reread the Student Model on page 101. Then answer the questions.
   1. Which sentence is out of order? Put a star next to it.
   2. Put ( ) around the sentence that ends the story.

B. Now evaluate the Student Model. Put a check in the box next to each thing the writer has done well. If you do not think the writer did a good job with something, do not check the box.

☐ The writer wrote a beginning that got the reader's attention.
☐ The writer used a clear beginning, middle, and ending.
☐ The writer included time-order words.
☐ The writer used *I, me,* and *my.*
☐ The writer described important things.

C. How do you think the writer could improve the story?

_____

_____

_____

_____

© Harcourt

See the rubric on page 207 for another way to evaluate the Student Model.

Name _____

Revise by Adding Time-Order Words

One thing the writer could have done better is to use time-order words in her story. Here is an example of how a sentence from the Student Model can be improved.

Example I went to a soccer game.

First, I went to a soccer game.
_____

A. Revise these sentences from the Student Model. Choose a time-order word from the box to add to each sentence.

last	next	then	later	the next day	in the morning

1. I saw Big Ben and heard it chime.

_____

_____

2. I rode on the biggest Ferris wheel in the world.

_____

_____

B. Revise the personal story you wrote on page 100. Use time-order words to make the order of events clear. Use another sheet of paper for more space.

_____

_____

_____

_____

© Harcourt

Writer's Companion • UNIT 4
Lesson 1 *A Good Beginning*

Name _____

Look at Audience and Purpose

Usually you write for people to read. The readers are your **audience.** When you write a letter, the audience is the person you are writing to. The reason you are writing something is called your **purpose.**

A. Read the following model. Notice the writer's audience and purpose.

Literature Model

Dear Aunt,

Captured by Cowboys.

Don't worry. See you soon.

Love,

Wallace

—from *How I Spent My Summer Vacation*
by Mark Teague

B Identify audience and purpose.
   1. Underline the audience for the letter.
   2. Circle the word that shows this is a friendly letter.

C. Wallace's purpose is to tell his aunt about something. What does he tell her?

_____

_____

_____

_____

© Harcourt

Name _____

Explore Audience and Purpose

The person you write to is called your audience. Your audience
for a friendly letter would be a friend or close relative. Your
audience for a formal letter would be a grown-up you do not
know very well, such as your teacher.

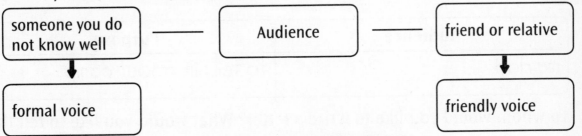

A. Read each letter. Then circle the kind of letter it is.

1. Dear Sir,

   Please leave the soccer field lights on later. We practice at 7:00.
   It is dark outside.

   Yours truly,

   John B.

   (formal letter)   friendly letter

2. Dear Sasha,

   I like my new school. The kids are pretty cool. But I miss you a lot.

   From, Anna

   formal letter   friendly letter

**B. Read this letter. Circle the audience. Then underline the sentence that
tells the purpose.**

Dear Mom,

I am having a great time at Aunt Meg's. We went to the museum yesterday.

Today we are going to the zoo.

Love,

Maya

**C. Change the letter in Part B into the formal voice. Use another sheet
of paper.**

© Harcourt

Name _____

Use Audience and Purpose

The purpose of a letter is to tell about something. The audience is the person the letter is written to. Here is how one student began to think about a letter.

Example

Audience	Purpose
my dad	to tell him about camp

A. To whom would you like to write a letter? What would you like to tell that person? Write your ideas in the chart.

Audience	Purpose

B. Use your chart to write the beginning of a friendly letter. If you need more space, use another sheet of paper.

_____

_____

_____

_____

© Harcourt

Name _____

The Parts of a Friendly Letter

A **friendly letter** has five parts. Here is a draft written by a second grader. Look at the parts of the letter as you read.

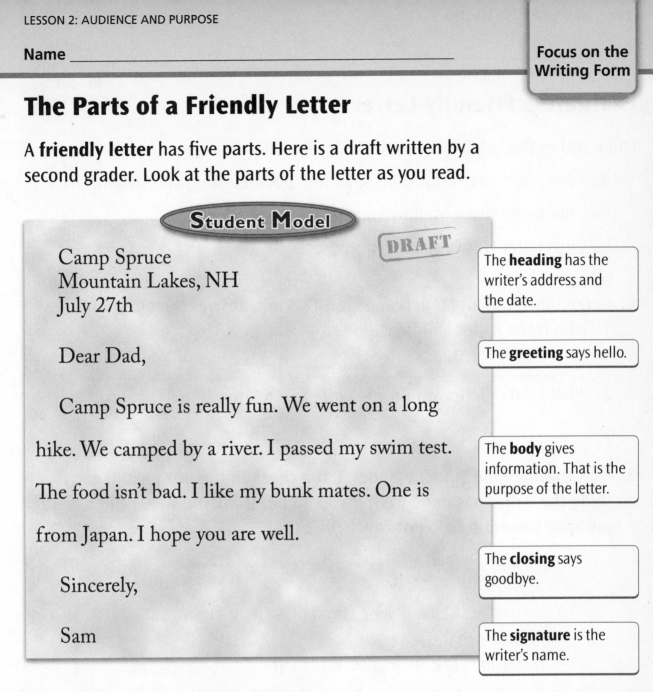

Student Model

DRAFT

Camp Spruce
Mountain Lakes, NH
July 27th

Dear Dad,

Camp Spruce is really fun. We went on a long hike. We camped by a river. I passed my swim test. The food isn't bad. I like my bunk mates. One is from Japan. I hope you are well.

Sincerely,

Sam

The **heading** has the writer's address and the date.

The **greeting** says hello.

The **body** gives information. That is the purpose of the letter.

The **closing** says goodbye.

The **signature** is the writer's name.

1. Underline the greeting in the letter.
2. Draw a circle around the closing of the letter.
3. Put a box around the heading of the letter.

Writer's Grammar
In a friendly letter, the greeting is followed by a comma. So is the closing. Find the commas after the greeting and closing in the Student Model.

© Harcourt

Name _____

Evaluate a Friendly Letter

When you evaluate a friendly letter, ask yourself:

- Does this letter have a heading, greeting, body, closing, and signature?
- Does the writer use a friendly voice and friendly words?
- Does this letter clearly state its purpose?

A. Reread the Student Model on page 107. Then answer the questions.

1. Who is the writer's audience?

_____

2. What kind of letter would you write to a relative?

_____

B. Now evaluate the Student Model. Put a check in the box next to each thing the writer has done well. If you do not think the writer did a good job with something, do not check the box.

☐ The writer used a heading, greeting, body, closing, and signature in the letter.

☐ The writer used the right kind of letter for the audience.

☐ The writer clearly stated the purpose of the letter.

C. How do you think the writer could improve the letter?

_____

_____

_____

_____

© Harcourt

See the rubric on page 207 for another way to evaluate the Student Model.

Name _____

Revise by Adding Friendlier Words

One thing the writer could do better is to use friendlier words.

Example The food isn't bad.

The food is pretty good!
_____

A. Revise these sentences from the Student Model. Use friendlier words.

1. I hope you are well.

_____

2. Sincerely,
Sam

_____

_____

B. Revise the beginning you wrote on page 106. Then finish the letter. Be sure to use friendly words.

_____

_____

_____

_____

_____

_____

_____

© Harcourt

Writer's Companion • UNIT 4
Lesson 2 *Audience and Purpose*

Name _____

Look at More About Audience and Purpose

The person you are writing to is your **audience.** The **purpose** is the reason you are writing.

A. Read the following model. The parts of the letter give clues about the voice.

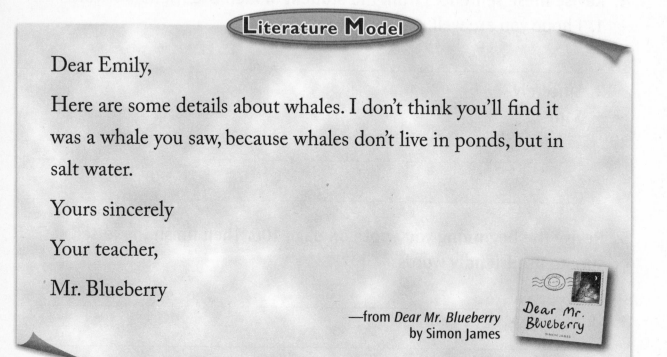

Literature Model

Dear Emily,

Here are some details about whales. I don't think you'll find it was a whale you saw, because whales don't live in ponds, but in salt water.

Yours sincerely

Your teacher,

Mr. Blueberry

—from *Dear Mr. Blueberry* by Simon James

B. Look at audience and purpose.
  1. To whom is the letter written? Circle the audience.
  2. Underline the sentence that tells the purpose of the letter.

C. Does Mr. Blueberry use a friendly or formal voice? _____

Which part of the letter tells you this? Box it.

© Harcourt

Name _____

Explore More About Audience and Purpose

Depending on the audience and purpose, your letter can be friendly or formal.

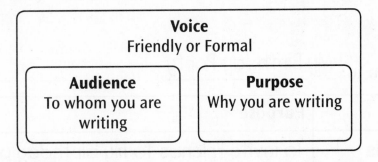

A. Read each invitation. Circle the audience. Then underline the purpose.

1. Dear (Ms. Nelson,)

   You are invited to a special teacher's class. The class is on November 2, at 11:00 a.m. I hope you can join us!

   Sincerely,

   Ann Baker

2. Dear Julia,

   I turn 8 tomorrow! I hope you can come to my birthday party. It is Saturday at 2:00 p.m. It is at the town pool. Bring your goggles!

   Love,

   Emma

B. Read this letter. Circle the audience and the closing. Then write whether the voice is formal or friendly.

Dear Mrs. Jackson,

The second grade is having an invention show. It will be on Monday at 9 a.m. Please come and see our inventions!

Sincerely, _____

Mr. Duffy's Grade 2 class

C. Rewrite the invitation in Part B. Invite a friend using a friendly voice. Use another sheet of paper.

© Harcourt

Name _____

Use More About Audience and Purpose

The purpose of a letter of invitation is to invite your audience to something. Here is how one student began to think about an invitation.

Example

An Invitation to: <u>My Birthday Party</u>

Audience	Purpose
My friends Voice: friendly	To invite friends to my birthday party

A. Think about a letter of invitation. Write the name of your event on the line. Then write the audience and the purpose. Write other details, too.

An Invitation to: _____

Audience	Purpose

B. Use the information from your chart to write a letter of invitation. Use another sheet of paper.

© Harcourt

Name _____

The Parts of a Letter of Invitation

A **letter of invitation** has the same five parts as a friendly letter. It also gives information about the people and event. Below is a first draft written by a second grader. As you read the invitation, look for details.

Student Model

DRAFT

154 N. 68th St.
Seattle, WA 98013

Dear Anika,

I am writing to ask you to come to my birthday

party! We will meet at the park first. Then we

will go out for Chinese food. I hope you can

come!

Your friend,

Megan

Who? asks, "Who are you inviting?"

What? asks, "What are you inviting people to?"

Why? asks, "Why is the event taking place?"

Where? asks, "Where is the event happening?"

When? asks, "When will the event take place?"

1. Underline the audience.
2. Circle the words that tell you what the audience is invited to.
3. Put a box around the closing of the letter of invitation.

Writer's Grammar
Pronouns are words that take the place of nouns. *I, me,* and *you* are some pronouns. Find pronouns in the Student Model.

Name _____

Evaluate a Letter of Invitation

When you evaluate a letter of invitation, ask yourself:

- Does this letter include a heading, greeting, body, closing, and signature?
- Does this letter use the right voice for the audience?
- Does this letter tell who, what, where, when, and why?

A. Reread the Student Model on page 113. Then answer the questions.
1. Who is giving the party?

_____

2. Is anything missing from the invitation? Explain

_____

B. Now evaluate the Student Model. Put a check in the box next to each thing the writer has done well. If you do not think the writer did a good job with something, do not check the box.

- ☐ The writer used a heading, greeting, body, closing, and signature.
- ☐ The writer used the right voice for the audience.
- ☐ The writer told who, what, where, when, and why in the letter.

C. How do you think the writer could improve the letter?

_____

_____

_____

_____

See the rubric on page 207 for another way to evaluate the Student Model.

© Harcourt

Name _____

Revise by Adding Details

One thing the student writer could have done better is to tell
exactly where and when the party is happening.

A. Write new details for the invitation. Tell where and when.

 1. Where?

 _____

 _____

 2. When?

 _____

 _____

B. Revise the letter of invitation you wrote on page 112. Be sure your letter
tells who, what, where, when, and why. If you need more space, use
another sheet of paper.

_____

_____

_____

_____

_____

_____

_____

_____

_____

© Harcourt

Name _____

Review Organization and Voice

A good beginning tells the reader what the story is about. A good
beginning makes the reader want to read more.

A. Read the beginning of this story.

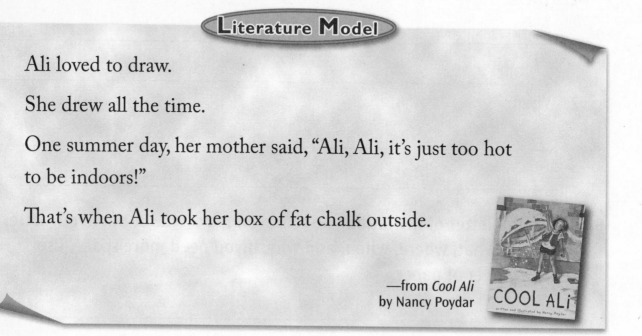

Literature Model

Ali loved to draw.

She drew all the time.

One summer day, her mother said, "Ali, Ali, it's just too hot
to be indoors!"

That's when Ali took her box of fat chalk outside.

—from *Cool Ali*
by Nancy Poydar

B. Look at a good beginning.
  1. Underline the sentences that begin the story.
  2. Circle a sentence that makes you want to read more.

C. Explain why the beginning of the story made you want to read more.

_____

_____

_____

© Harcourt

Name _____

Review Organization and Voice

The person you are writing to is your **audience**. The **purpose** is why you write. The **voice** depends on audience and purpose.

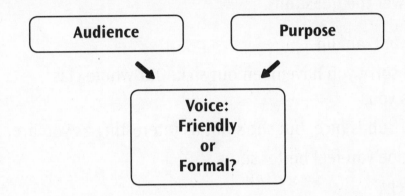

Audience

Purpose

**Voice:
Friendly
or
Formal?**

A. Read the following letter from *Dear Mr. Blueberry*. Then answer the questions.

> Dear Mr. Blueberry,
>
> Last night I read your letter to my whale. Afterward he let me stroke his head. It was very exciting.
>
> I secretly took him some crunched-up cornflakes and bread crumbs. This morning I looked in the pond and they were all gone!
>
> I think I shall call him Arthur.
> What do you think?
>
> Love,
> Emily

B. Write your answers on the lines.

1. Who is the audience? _____

2. What kind of voice does Emily use? _____

C. What is the purpose of Emily's letter? Explain.

_____

Name _____

Review Organization and Voice

The **voice** of your letter can be friendly or formal. The voice you choose depends on **audience** and **purpose**. Read this formal letter and answer the questions.

> Dear Mr. Franklin,
>
> I'm sorry you have been out sick. Our whole class misses you.
>
> Our sub is nice, but she's not as interesting as you are.
>
> I hope you feel better soon.
>
> Sincerely,
>
> Angela Leoni

A. Write your answers on the lines.

1. Who is the audience of the letter? _____

2. What is the purpose of the letter? _____

_____

B. Rewrite the same letter to a classmate. Change the voice from formal to friendly. If you need more space, use another sheet of paper.

_____

_____

_____

_____

_____

_____

© Harcourt

Name _____

The Parts of a Personal Story

A **personal story** tells about an event in the writer's life. It has a beginning, a middle, and an ending. Below is a draft written by a second grader. As you read, think about the story's beginning and purpose.

Student Model

DRAFT

My Sleepy Morning
by Ari

Yesterday, my alarm did not go off. I woke up very late. I grabbed my book bag and a bagel. I threw on my jacket and just made it to the school bus. Then I realized two things. My hair was a mess, and I was still wearing my pajama top! How dumb is that? I had to wear my jacket all day. I was sure glad when school was over!

> A good **beginning** makes the reader want to read more. It also tells the **purpose** of the story.

> The action in the story happens in the **middle**.

> The **ending** of the story should wrap up the action.

1. Underline a good beginning sentence.
2. What is the writer's purpose?

_____

_____

Writer's Grammar
A sentence can be long or short. Find long and short sentences in the story.

© Harcourt

Name _____

Evaluate a Personal Story

A. Two students wrote personal stories. The story below got a score of 4. A score of 4 means excellent. As you read, think about the teacher's notes.

Student Model

DRAFT

**Bruno Goes to School
by Ella**

Yesterday was the funniest day I've ever had at school. We were at our all-school meeting. The principal announced the birthdays. While he was talking, we heard an oink. Then we heard a snort. Kids started giggling. Teachers started looking around. Suddenly a girl jumped up as a little pink pig ran right over her lap! Everyone was laughing and grabbing at the pig. Max, a third grader, had brought his pig Bruno in for Cool Week. I guess Bruno felt lonely in the classroom. He decided to come to the meeting and have some fun!

> Good job! Your beginning is interesting and makes me want to keep reading. It also states the **purpose** of the story.

> The middle section of your story has the action.

> Nice ending to your story. It really wraps everything up well!

© Harcourt

Name _____

B. This paragraph got a score of 2. Why did it get a low score?

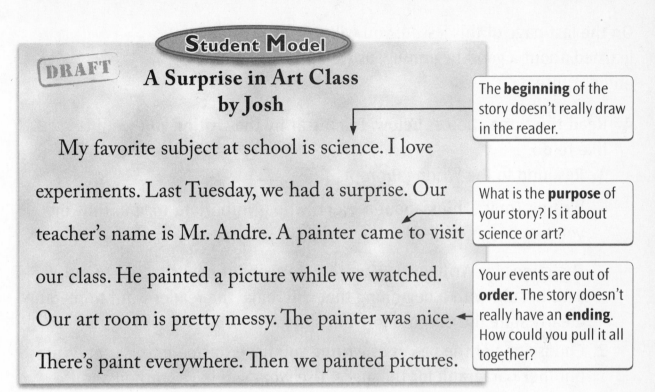

Student Model

DRAFT

**A Surprise in Art Class
by Josh**

My favorite subject at school is science. I love

experiments. Last Tuesday, we had a surprise. Our

teacher's name is Mr. Andre. A painter came to visit

our class. He painted a picture while we watched.

Our art room is pretty messy. The painter was nice.

There's paint everywhere. Then we painted pictures.

> The **beginning** of the story doesn't really draw in the reader.

> What is the **purpose** of your story? Is it about science or art?

> Your events are out of **order**. The story doesn't really have an **ending**. How could you pull it all together?

C. What score would you give the student's story? Put a number on each line.

	4	3	2	1
Organization/ Paragraphs _____	☐ The story tells the events in the correct order.	☐ The story tells the events in order most of the time.	☐ The story does not tell the events in order in some places.	☐ The story does not tell the events in order at all.
Voice _____	☐ The writer's voice is very clear.	☐ The writer's voice is pretty clear.	☐ The writer's voice is not very clear.	☐ The writer's voice is not clear at all.
Focus/Ideas _____	☐ The purpose of the story is very clear.	☐ The purpose of the story is pretty clear.	☐ The purpose of the story is not so clear.	☐ The purpose of the story is not clear at all.

Extended Writing/Test Prep

On the last page of this lesson, you will use what you have learned about a good beginning, as well as voice, audience, and purpose.

A. **Read the three choices below. Put a star by the writing you would like to do.**

1. Respond to the Writing Prompt.

Writing Topic: Think about a friend who is important to you. How did you two become friends?

Directions for Writing: Now write a story about meeting that friend. Be sure to start with a beginning that will make the reader want to read on. Clearly state the purpose for your story.

2. Choose one of the pieces of writing you have started in this unit. Write another paragraph for the piece. Use what you have learned about beginning a story, as well as voice, audience, and purpose in a story or letter.

- a personal story (page 100)
- a friendly letter (page 106)
- a letter of invitation (page 112)

3. Choose a new topic and write a personal story. Be sure to include a good beginning, a middle, and an ending.

B. Use the space below to plan your writing.

TOPIC: _____

WRITING FORM: _____

HOW WILL I ORGANIZE MY WRITING: _____

_____

© Harcourt

Name _____

C. In the space below, draw a graphic organizer that will help you plan your writing. Fill in the graphic organizer. Write more notes on the lines below.

Notes

_____

_____

_____

_____

_____

_____

_____

D. Use another sheet of paper for your writing.

Name _____

Answering Multiple-Choice Questions

Some writing tests have questions with answer choices. This lesson will help you practice this kind of test.

A. Some test questions may ask you to read three sentences and decide which is correct. Read the test tip and the questions.

Answer questions 1–4 on the Answer Sheet.

1. In which pair of sentences is the **pronoun** correct?
   A   Lara is hungry. She wants to eat lunch.
   B   Eddie is tired. They is happy to be home.
   C   Sal and I ran fast. Them are tired.

2. In which pair of sentences is the **pronoun** correct?
   F   Milo and Tim are good soccer players. He is fast.
   G   The book is heavy. It weighs three pounds.
   H   That scarf looks warm. She is made of wool.

> **Test Tip:**
> Pronouns take the place of nouns. *I, you, he, she, it, we,* and *they* are some pronouns.

3. Which sentence is correct?
   A   Marc run a race.
   B   Marc rans a race.
   C   Marc ran a race.

4. In which sentence is all **capitalization** correct?
   F   My friend Jenny gave John a gift.
   G   My friend Jenny gave john a gift.
   H   My friend jenny gave john a gift.

Answer all test questions on this Answer Sheet.

1. (A) (B) (C)   3. (A) (B) (C)

2. (F) (G) (H)   4. (F) (G) (H)

Name _____

B. For some multiple-choice questions, you will have to read a sentence and tell what type of word is underlined. Read the test tip. Mark your answers on the Answer Sheet.

1. Read this sentence.

There <u>is</u> a <u>small</u> yo-yo in the <u>old</u> toy <u>chest</u>.

In this sentence, which underlined word tells about size?

A is

B small

C old

D chest

2. Read this sentence.

There <u>is</u> a <u>red</u> <u>ball</u> in the <u>hot</u> road.

In this sentence, which underlined word tells about color?

F is   H ball

G red   I hot

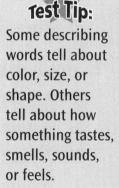

Test Tip:
Some describing words tell about color, size, or shape. Others tell about how something tastes, smells, sounds, or feels.

3. Read this sentence.

A <u>little</u> <u>yellow</u> whistle makes a <u>loud</u> toot when you <u>blow</u> into it.

In this sentence, which underlined word tells about how something sounds?

A little   C loud

B yellow   D blow

Answer all test questions on this Answer Sheet.

1. (A) (B) (C) (D)   3. (A) (B) (C) (D)

2. (F) (G) (H) (I)

© Harcourt

Name _____

C. Some test questions may ask you to read four sentences and decide which one is correct. Read the test tip. Then practice answering this type of question.

Read and answer each question on the Answer Sheet.

1. Which sentence is written correctly?

   A   There were one apples on the tree.

   B   There were most apples on the tree.

   C   There were many apples on the tree.

   D   There were two apple on the tree.

2. Which sentence is written correctly?

   F   A human has many eye.

   G   A human has two eyes.

   H   A human has most eye.

   I   A human has one eyes.

3. Which sentence is written correctly?

   A   The fire alarm rang for three minutes.

   B   The fire alarm rang for most minute.

   C   The fire alarm rang for all minute.

   D   The fire alarm rang for one minutes.

4. Which sentence is written correctly?

   F   We will go back to the pool in all weeks.

   G   We will go back to the pool in one weeks.

   H   We will go back to the pool in most week.

   I   We will go back to the pool in two weeks.

> **Test Tip:**
> Number words, like *two*, *six*, or *all*, tell exactly how many. Other words like *some*, *many*, or *few*, give an idea of how many.

Answer all test questions on this Answer Sheet.

1.   Ⓐ   Ⓑ   Ⓒ   Ⓓ   3.   Ⓐ   Ⓑ   Ⓒ   Ⓓ

2.   Ⓕ   Ⓖ   Ⓗ   Ⓘ   4.   Ⓕ   Ⓖ   Ⓗ   Ⓘ

Name _____

D. For some multiple-choice questions, you will have to read a passage and then decide which word best completes a sentence. Read the test tip. Then fill in the circle next to the answer.

Read the story "The Very Bad Day." Choose the words that correctly complete questions 1–4.

The Very Bad Day

Today felt like the ___(1)___ day I've ever had. My cat ran away this morning. I spilled my juice at lunch. It made a ___(2)___ mess than I've made in a while. I had a ___(3)___ spelling test this afternoon. Then, my sister got ___(4)___ at me for borrowing her bike. I can't wait to wake up tomorrow. I know it will be better!

1. Which answer should go in blank (1)?

   Ⓐ long

   Ⓑ longer

   Ⓒ longest

2. Which answer should go in blank (2)?

   Ⓕ big

   Ⓖ bigger

   Ⓗ biggest

3. Which answer should go in blank (3)?

   Ⓐ hard

   Ⓑ harder

   Ⓒ hardest

4. Which answer should go in blank (4)?

   Ⓕ mad

   Ⓖ madder

   Ⓗ maddest

> **Test Tip:**
> A describing word that ends with *–er* compares one thing with another thing. A describing word that ends with *–est* compares one thing with two or more things.

© Harcourt

Name _____

Look at What Something is Like

When writers describe, they tell what a person, place, or thing is like. Writers use words that help readers **see, hear, taste, smell,** and **feel.**

A. Read the following Literature Model. Look for words that describe.

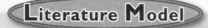

Miss Rosa: *(gasps)* That's Dynah! She's my new pet mynah bird. She escaped from the bookstore this morning. I've been looking for her all day! *(looks at Lan and Jeff)* How did you two know Dynah was the thief?

Lan: Jeff figured out that all the missing objects were small and shiny, so we decided to set a trap.

—from *The Pine Park Mystery*
by Tracey West

B. Identify words that describe.

   1. Underline the word that helps you hear something.

   2. Circle two words that help you see what something is like.

C. What kind of bird is Dynah?

_____

© Harcourt

Name _____

Explore What Something is Like

A **simile** is a special kind of description. It tells how two different things are alike. Similes often use the words *like* or *as* to compare.

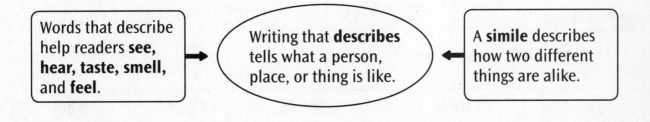

Words that describe help readers **see, hear, taste, smell,** and **feel**. → Writing that **describes** tells what a person, place, or thing is like. ← A **simile** describes how two different things are alike.

A. Underline the two things that are compared in each simile.

Example The buttons are as bright as stars.

1. The feathers are as white as snow.

2. The drums sound like thunder.

B. Read this sentence about *The Pine Park Mystery*. Circle the two things that are compared.

The boys had to think like real detectives.

C. Complete the simile.

The girl swam like a _____.

Name _____

Use What Something Is Like

Writers sometimes plan how they will describe their topic. They use words that tell what they see, hear, smell, taste, and feel. Here is what one student wrote about eating in the school lunchroom.

Example **Topic Sentence:** _Today I ate lunch in the school lunchroom for the first time._

See	Hear	Smell	Taste	Feel
• shiny, brown tray	• laughing • chattering	• peeled orange, fresh smell	• juicy hotdog	• hot soup

A. Choose a place where you have eaten. Write a topic sentence. Then list words that describe your topic.

Topic Sentence: _____

See	Hear	Smell	Taste	Feel

B. Now use words from your chart to write a paragraph. Do your writing on another sheet of paper.

© Harcourt

Name _____

The Parts of a Paragraph That Describes

A **paragraph that describes** has two parts. It has a topic sentence and detail sentences with describing words. Below is a draft written by a second grader. As you read, think about the topic and describing words. Then answer the questions.

Student Model

DRAFT

Lunch at School
by Rudy

Today I ate lunch in the school lunchroom for the first time. Kids were laughing and chattering. I carried my lunch on a shiny, brown tray. I sat with my friend who was peeling an orange. It had a nice fresh smell. I sipped my hot vegetable soup. Then I ate a juicy hotdog and chips. I ate some sliced peaches, too.

> The **topic sentence** tells what the paragraph is about.

> Describing words in detail sentences help readers **see, hear, smell, taste,** and **feel** what things are like.

1. Which sentence tells the topic? Put a box around it.

2. Which detail sentence helps the reader hear something? Circle it.

3. Which detail names something that smells nice? Put [ ] around it.

4. Which detail helps the reader taste something. Draw a line under it.

Writer's Grammar
Some words tell what happened in the past. Find an example in the Student Model of a word that tells what happened in the past.

© Harcourt

Name _____

Evaluate a Paragraph That Describes

When you study a paragraph that describes, ask yourself these questions:

- Does the writer tell you what will be described?
  (Look for the topic sentence.)

- Does the writer paint a picture of things?
  (Look for detail sentences.)

- Does the writer use words that help you see, hear, taste, smell, and feel?
  (Look for describing words.)

A. Reread the Student Model on page 131. Then answer these questions.

1. Which sentence paints a picture of something the writer carried?

_____

2. What word helps you taste the hotdog? _____

B. Now evaluate the Student Model. Put a check in the box next to each thing the writer has done well. If you do not think the writer did a good job with something, do not check the box.

☐ The topic sentence tells what the paragraph is about.
☐ The writer told what a person, place, or thing is like.
☐ The writer used describing words that help you see, hear, smell, taste, and feel.

C. How do you think the writer could make the paragraph better? Write your ideas below.

_____

_____

© Harcourt

Writer's Companion • UNIT 5
Lesson 1 *What Something Is Like*

132

See the rubric on page 207 for another way to evaluate the Student Model.

Name _____

Revise a Paragraph That Describes

One way the writer could make the paragraph better is to add describing words. The writer could also add a simile. Here is an example of a simile that can be added to the Student Model.

Example The sliced peaches looked like smiles.

A. Revise the Student Model by adding a simile and describing word. Use the Word Bank for ideas.

1. The chattering sounded like _____.

2. Then I ate a juicy hotdog and _____ chips.

B. Revise your paragraph on page 130. Add describing words and a simile. If you need more space, use another sheet of paper.

> **Word Bank**
> birds
> bees
> chirping
> buzzing
> salty
> crunchy
> _____
> _____

_____

_____

_____

_____

_____

_____

_____

_____

© Harcourt

Name _____

Look at Rhyme and Rhythm

Writing can have a **rhythm**. This rhythm is made by the pattern of repeated beats, or syllables, and words.

A. Read the following Literature Model aloud softly. Listen for the rhythm.

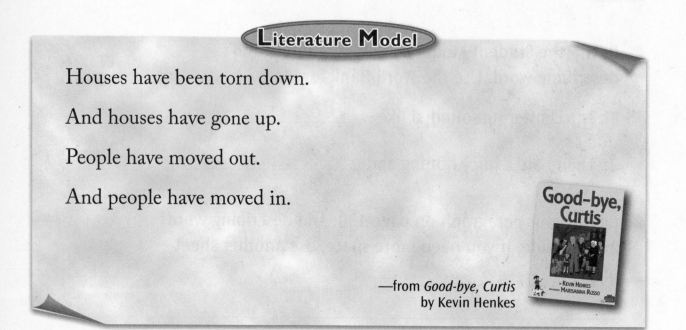

Literature Model

Houses have been torn down.

And houses have gone up.

People have moved out.

And people have moved in.

—from *Good-bye, Curtis*
by Kevin Henkes

B. Identify the rhythm.

   1. Put a dot over each beat, or syllable, in the first two sentences. What is the pattern?

      _____beats in each sentence

   2. Circle the repeated words in the last two sentences.

C. Look at each pair of lines in the poem. What kind of words are

down/up and *out/in?* _____

Name _____

Explore Rhyme and Rhythm

In a poem, a writer describes something in an interesting way. A poem has a rhythm. Some words in a poem can **rhyme**.

A poem has a **title** that tells what the poem is about.	A poem has a rhythm of **repeated** words or **number of beats.**	A poem has **describing** words. It can have **rhyming** words.

A. Read the lines from poems. Underline repeated words. Put a box around rhyming words.

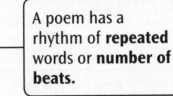

Example My black kitten likes to jump.
My black rabbit likes to thump.

1. He rushed to the wall,
   And he caught the ball!
   For him it was a great play,
   For fans it was a great day.

2. See the rain over the lake,
   Drop, drop, drop.
   Hear the rain in the lake,
   Plop, plop, plop.

B. Read the following. Write another line to make a poem.

The sky is very dark tonight.

_____

© Harcourt

Name _____

Use Rhyme and Rhythm

Before writing a poem, writers often list describing words they want to use. Some may be rhyming words. This is what one student wrote about seagulls.

Example **Title of Poem:** _Gulls by the Sea_____

Describing Words	Rhyming Words
• white body, some gray feathers • black tips on wings • black head • red beak and feet	• stand, sand • cry, fly • sea, free

A. Think about a bird you like. Then fill in the chart.

Title of Poem: _____

Describing Words	Rhyming Words

B. Now use words from your chart to write a poem. Do your writing on another sheet of paper.

Name _____

The Parts of a Poem That Uses Rhyme and Rhythm

A **poem that uses rhyme and rhythm** has some words that rhyme. It also has a pattern of repeated words or beats. Below is a poem that uses rhyme and rhythm written by a second grader. As you read, think about how the student used rhyme and rhythm.

Student Model

DRAFT

Gulls by the Sea
by Ella

White birds on the sand,

There they stand.

Beak and feet red,

Black on the head.

I hear them cry,

Away they fly.

The gulls are flying free.

They fly by the sea.

> The **title** tells what the poem is about.

> The poem has **rhyming words**.

> The poem has **rhythm**: mostly 4 beats to each line.

1. What is the poem about? Circle the topic.

2. Put a box around a pair of lines with 4 beats in each line.

Writer's Grammar
Writers use a comma (,) to show readers when to pause. Find the commas in the Student Model.

© Harcourt

137

Name _____

Evaluate a Poem That Uses Rhyme and Rhythm

When you study a poem that uses rhyme and rhythm, ask yourself these questions:

- Does the writer use describing words?
  (Look for words that paint a picture.)

- Does the writer use rhyming words?
  (Look at the ends of lines for words that sound the same.)

- Does the poem have rhythm?
  (Listen for repeated words or number of beats.)

A. Reread the Student Model on page 137. Then answer these questions.
   1. What word describes a gull's beak and feet?

   _____

   2. Write two pairs of words that rhyme.

   _____

B. Now evaluate the Student Model. Put a check in the box next to each thing the writer has done well. If you do not think the writer did a good job with something, do not check the box.

☐ The writer used describing words.
☐ The writer used rhyming words.
☐ The poem has a rhythm.

C. How do you think the writer could make the poem better? Write your ideas below.

_____

_____

See the rubric on page 207 for another way to evaluate the Student Model.

© Harcourt

Name _____

Revise a Poem That Uses Rhyme and Rhythm

One thing the writer could have done is use lines of different lengths. The writer could also have added rhythm. Here is an example of how short lines can be used in the Student Model and how they add rhythm.

Word Bank

birds
high
sky
up
white
_____
_____

Example The gulls are flying free.

Flying free
_____

They fly by the sea.

By the sea
_____

A. Revise the Student Model by adding a pair of lines that have the same rhythm as the first two lines. Use the Word Bank for ideas.

1. _____.

2. _____

B. Revise your poem on page 136. Add shorter or longer lines, and add rhythm. If you need more space, use another sheet of paper.

_____

_____

_____

_____

_____

_____

Writer's Companion • UNIT 5
Lesson 2 *Rhyme and Rhythm*

Name _____

Look at Rhythm and Rhyme

Many poets do not use rhyme. They use **rhythm**, or **beat**, and sometimes **sound words** to make their poems fun to read.

A. Read the following Literature Model aloud softly. Listen for the rhythm and sound words.

Literature Model

> Max answered on the bottles,
>
> *Dong . . . dang . . . dung.*
>
> *Ding . . . dong . . . ding!*
>
> His music joined the chiming of the bells in the church around the corner.
>
> —from *Max Found Two Sticks*
> by Brian Pinkney

B. Identify the sound words and rhythm.

   1. Underline the sound words.

   2. How many beats are in each line of sound words? _____

C. Why are the sound words fun to read?

   _____

   _____

   _____

   _____

© Harcourt

Name _____

Explore Rhythm and Rhyme

A poem does not have to have rhyming words. Writers can use **sound words**. Sound words have a rhythm.

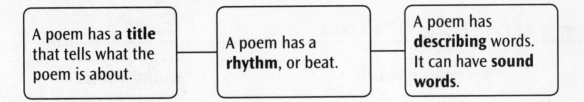

A poem has a **title** that tells what the poem is about.

A poem has a **rhythm**, or beat.

A poem has **describing** words. It can have **sound words**.

A. Underline the sound words. Listen to the rhythm.

> **Example** There's an old <u>clock</u> on the wall,
> <u>Tick-tick-tock</u>, <u>tock-tock-tick</u>.

1. My dog wants to walk,
   Arf-arf, arf-arf-arf at me.

2. Ah-choo, I have a cold.
   Ah-CHOO, to bed I go.

B. Read this sentence from *Max Found Two Sticks*. Underline the sound words.

> He just played on the boxes, *Dum … dum-de-dum.*

C. Use sound words to write a sentence about a train.
Repeat the words to create a rhythm.

_____

_____

Name _____

Use Rhythm and Rhyme

Before you write a poem, think of a topic and a title. Then list describing words and sound words to use in your poem. Here is what one student wrote about a pond.

Example **Title of Poem:** The Pond

Describing Words	Sound Words
• frogs, big eyes • bugs • ducks, green heads • beavers, flat tails	• glump • bizz • quack • flap

A. Write down a title for a poem about things you hear in a place you have been. Then fill in the chart.

Title of Poem: _____

Describing Words	Sound Words

B. Now use words from your chart to write a poem. Use another sheet of paper for your writing.

© Harcourt

Name _____

A Poem with Rhythm

A **poem with rhythm** has a pattern of words. It may use sound words instead of rhyming words. Below is a poem with rhythm written by a second grader. As you read, think about describing words and sound words.

Student Model

DRAFT

**The Pond
by Luis**

Frogs with big eyes,

Glump, glump, glump.

Bugs with wings,

Bizz-bizz, bizz-bizz.

Ducks with green heads,

Quack, quack, quack.

Beavers with flat tails,

Flap-flap, flap-flap.

Birds with black feathers.

The **title** tells what the poem is about.

Sound words give the poem **rhythm**.

The poem has **describing words**.

1. What words describe what the birds look like? Put a box around them.
2. What words describe the sound bugs make? Underline them.

© Harcourt

Writer's Grammar
Writers often make up words for sounds. Look for a made-up sound word in the Student Model.

143

Name _____

Evaluate a Poem with Rhythm

When you study a poem with rhythm, ask yourself
these questions:

- Does the writer use describing words?
  (Look for words that paint a picture.)

- Does the writer use sound words?
  (Listen for words that tell about sounds.)

- Does the poem have rhythm?
  (Listen for beats.)

A. **Reread the Student Model on page 143. Then answer these questions.**
  1. What sound words have the same beats as *Bizz-bizz, bizz-bizz?*

  _____

  2. What describing words paint a picture of the ducks?

  _____

B. **Now evaluate the Student Model. Put a check in the box next to each
thing the writer has done well. If you do not think the writer did a good
job with something, do not check the box.**

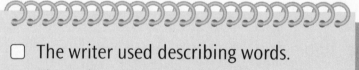

☐ The writer used describing words.
☐ The writer used sound words.
☐ The poem has a rhythm.

C. **How do you think the writer could make the poem better? Write your
ideas below.**

_____

_____

Writer's Companion • UNIT 5
Lesson 3 *Rhythm and Rhyme*

144

See the rubric on page 207 for another
way to evaluate the Student Model.

© Harcourt

Name _____

Revise a Poem with Rhythm

Something the writer could have done better is use more
describing and sound words. Here is an example of describing
and sound words that can be added to the Student Model.

Example Bugs with ____*clear*____ wings
_____

Birds with black feathers,
___*Chee, chee, chee*___.

**Word
Bank**

tiny

long

caw

_____

_____

A. Revise the Student Model by adding a describing word and
sound words. Use the Word Bank for ideas.

1. Bugs with _____ wings.

2. Birds with black feathers,

_____

B. Revise your poem on page 142. Add describing and sound words.

_____

_____

_____

_____

_____

_____

_____

© Harcourt

Writer's Companion • UNIT 5
Lesson 3 *Rhythm and Rhyme*

Name _____

Review Word Choice and Sentence Fluency

Some writing tells about something that really happened.
The writer gives a strong description of how things **look, feel,
sound, smell,** and **taste**. The writer may use **sound words**.

A. Read the following Literature Model. Look for words that describe.

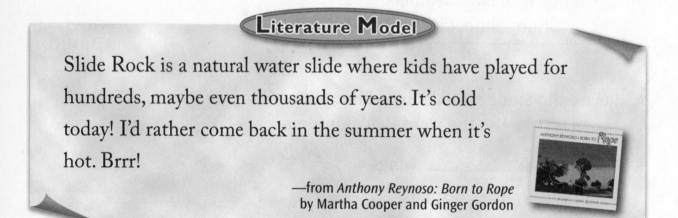

Literature Model

Slide Rock is a natural water slide where kids have played for
hundreds, maybe even thousands of years. It's cold
today! I'd rather come back in the summer when it's
hot. Brrr!

—from *Anthony Reynoso: Born to Rope*
by Martha Cooper and Ginger Gordon

B. Identify the describing words.

1. What words describe what Slide Rock looks like? Put a box around
   the words.

2. What describing word and sound word tell what the water feels like?
   Circle these words.

C. Why does Anthony like Slide Rock better in the summer?

_____

_____

Name _____

Review Word Choice and Sentence Fluency

Rhyming words and **repeated** words and sounds give writing a **rhythm**.

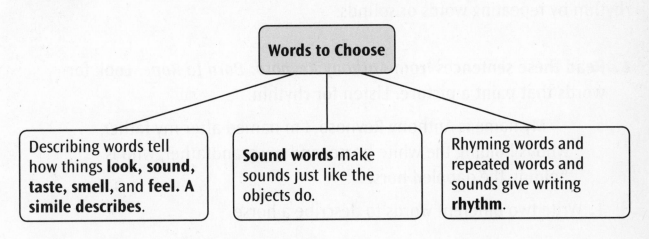

Words to Choose

Describing words tell how things **look, sound, taste, smell,** and **feel**. A **simile describes**.

Sound words make sounds just like the objects do.

Rhyming words and repeated words and sounds give writing **rhythm**.

A. Read the poem. Look for words that give the poem rhythm.

> I biked like a rocket to the park.
> I played in the park with Mike.
> We swung on the swing.
> We heard robins sing.
> We slid on the slide.
> We saw chipmunks hide.

B. Write the words that give the poem rhythm.

Example Rhyming words: _swing, sing_____

Repeated words or sounds: _swung, swing_____

1. More rhyming words: _____

2. Simile: _____

C. Read this sentence from *Anthony Reynoso: Born to Rope*. Underline words with repeated sounds that give the writing rhythm.

> We all rope and ride Mexican Rodeo style on my grandfather's ranch outside of Phoenix, Arizona.

© Harcourt

Name _____

Review Word Choice and Sentence Fluency

When you write a story, use words that describe how things
look, sound, taste, smell, and **feel.** Try to give your writing
rhythm by repeating words or sounds.

A. Read these sentences from *Anthony Reynoso: Born to Rope.* Look for
words that paint a picture. Listen for rhythm.

> My name is Anthony Reynoso. I'm named after my father,
> who is holding the white horse, and my grandfather, who is
> holding the dappled horse.

1. Write two different words to describe a horse.

_____

_____

2. Write the repeated words that give rhythm.

_____

_____

B. Write your own words to describe how horses look, feel, and sound.

Look: _____

_____

Feel: _____

_____

Sound: _____

_____

© Harcourt

Name _____

The Parts of a Personal Story

In a **personal story**, a writer tells about something that really happened. A personal story tells how the writer feels about what happened. The writer describes how things look, sound, taste, smell, and feel. The writer uses words like *I, me,* and *my.*

A. Below is a draft written by a second grader. As you read, think about the words the writer uses to describe things. Then answer the questions.

Student Model

The Clown at My Birthday Party
by Jenny

DRAFT

My last birthday was fun. There was a clown with purple hair on my cake. The cake was yummy! The purple hair tasted like sweet grapes. A real clown was supposed to come to my party, but he was sick.

> The writer tells the problem.

> The writer uses describing words.

I opened a present. It was soap shaped like a lemon. It felt bumpy like a lemon and smelled like one. Then I heard HONK! I laughed. I saw a clown wave at me. It was Dad! I was a happy birthday girl.

> The writer tells how the problem is solved.

> The writer tells how she feels.

1. Underline the word that describes how the soap felt.
2. Put a box around the word that describes the sound of the horn.
3. Does the writer use words like *I, me,* and *my?* Circle them.

Writer's Grammar
When you write a story, indent each paragraph. Leave space for about three letters. Then begin the first word of the paragraph. Find each paragraph indent in the Student Model.

Name _____

Evaluating a Personal Story

A. Two students wrote a personal story about a special birthday. The story below got a score of 4. A score of 4 means excellent. As you read, think about the teacher's notes.

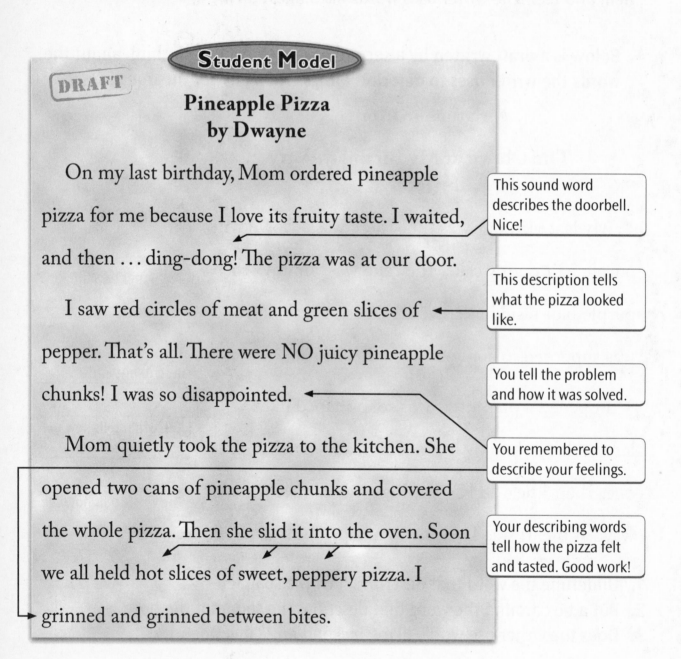

Student Model

DRAFT

Pineapple Pizza
by Dwayne

On my last birthday, Mom ordered pineapple pizza for me because I love its fruity taste. I waited, and then ... ding-dong! The pizza was at our door.

> This sound word describes the doorbell. Nice!

I saw red circles of meat and green slices of pepper. That's all. There were NO juicy pineapple chunks! I was so disappointed.

> This description tells what the pizza looked like.

> You tell the problem and how it was solved.

Mom quietly took the pizza to the kitchen. She opened two cans of pineapple chunks and covered the whole pizza. Then she slid it into the oven. Soon we all held hot slices of sweet, peppery pizza. I grinned and grinned between bites.

> You remembered to describe your feelings.

> Your describing words tell how the pizza felt and tasted. Good work!

© Harcourt

Name _____

B. **This paragraph got a score of 2. Why did it get a low score?**

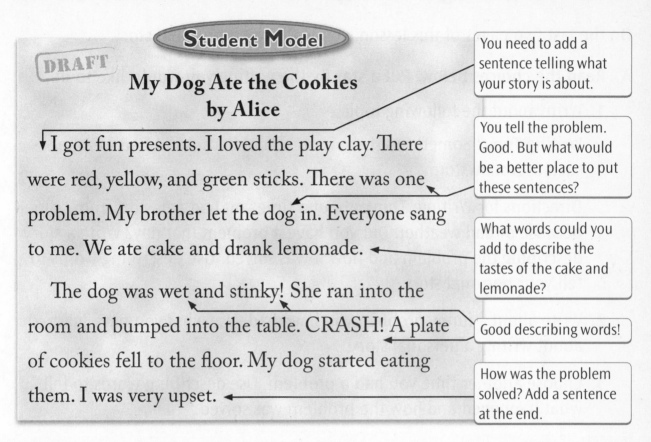

Student Model

DRAFT

My Dog Ate the Cookies
by Alice

I got fun presents. I loved the play clay. There were red, yellow, and green sticks. There was one problem. My brother let the dog in. Everyone sang to me. We ate cake and drank lemonade.

The dog was wet and stinky! She ran into the room and bumped into the table. CRASH! A plate of cookies fell to the floor. My dog started eating them. I was very upset.

You need to add a sentence telling what your story is about.

You tell the problem. Good. But what would be a better place to put these sentences?

What words could you add to describe the tastes of the cake and lemonade?

Good describing words!

How was the problem solved? Add a sentence at the end.

C. **What score would you give the student's story? Put a number on each line.**

	4	3	2	1
Focus/Ideas _____	☐ The topic of the story is very clear.	☐ The topic of the story is clear.	☐ The topic of the story is not so clear.	☐ The topic of the story is not clear at all.
Organization/ Paragraphs _____	☐ The story tells events in order. The paragraphs are indented.	☐ The story tells the events in order most of the time.	☐ The events are not told in order in some places.	☐ The story does not tell the events in order at all.
Word Choice _____	☐ Describing words and details are used to tell the story.	☐ Some describing words and details are used to tell the story.	☐ More describing words and details are needed.	☐ There are no describing words or details.

© Harcourt

Writer's Companion ▪ UNIT 5
Lesson 4 *Review Word Choice and Sentence Fluency*

Name _____

Extended Writing/Test Prep

On the last two pages of this lesson, you will write a personal story.

A. **Read the choices below. Put a star by the writing you would like to do.**

1. Write about the following topic.

Writing Topic: Sometimes there is no school because of bad weather, such as a snowstorm.

Directions for Writing: Think about a time you had a day off from school because of bad weather. Did you have a problem that day? Write a story describing the problem and how it was solved. Use describing words to tell your personal story.

2. Write about a funny problem you have had. Use what you have learned about writing a personal story.

3. Choose another time you had a problem. Use describing words to tell what happened and how the problem was solved.

B. **Use the space below to plan your writing.**

TOPIC: _____

PROBLEM: _____

HOW PROBLEM WAS SOLVED: _____

_____

_____

DESCRIBING WORDS: _____

_____

_____

Name _____

C. In the space below, draw a chart that will help you plan your writing. Fill in the chart. Write notes on the lines below.

Notes

_____

_____

_____

_____

_____

_____

_____

_____

D. Write at least two paragraphs about your topic on another sheet of paper.

Writer's Companion • UNIT 5
Lesson 4 *Review Word Choice
and Sentence Fluency*

© Harcourt

Name _____

Answering Multiple-Choice Questions

Some writing tests have questions with answer choices. This lesson will help you answer different kinds of questions often found in writing tests.

A. For some questions, you will have to decide the best way to write a sentence. Read the test tip. Then answer this kind of question.

Read and answer each question. Mark your answers on the Answer Sheet.

1. What is the correct way to write the sentence?

    A Now he looking out the window.

    B Now he look out the window.

    C Now he looks out the window.

    D Now he looking out the window.

2. What is the correct way to write the sentence?

    A He watches the snowflakes fall.

    B He watch the snowflakes falls.

    C He watch the snowflakes falling.

    D He watch the snowflakes fall.

> **Test Tip:**
> Be sure to read all of the choices before marking your answer.

3. What is the correct way to write the sentence?

    A As the snowflakes fall, the cat rubbed the glass with its paw.

    B As the snowflakes falls, the cat rubs the glass with its paw.

    C As the snowflakes falled, the cat rubs the glass with its paw.

    D As the snowflakes fall, the cat rubs the glass with its paw.

© Harcourt

Answer all test questions on this Answer Sheet.

1. Ⓐ Ⓑ Ⓒ Ⓓ   3. Ⓐ Ⓑ Ⓒ Ⓓ

2. Ⓐ Ⓑ Ⓒ Ⓓ

Name _____

B. For some questions, you will have to read three or four sentences, and decide which sentence is correctly written. Read the test tip. Then answer this kind of question.

Read and answer questions 1–4 below. Fill in the circle next to your answer choice.

1. Which sentence below is correct?

(A) The frog eat bugs.

(B) The frog eats bugs.

(C) The frogs eats bugs.

2. Which sentence below is correct?

(F) A leaf falls to the ground.

(G) A leaf fall to the ground.

(H) Leaves falls to the ground.

> **Test Tip:**
> The letter *s* is at the end of some verbs that tell about now. There is no letter *s* if the verb is used with *I, you,* or more than one person.

3. Which sentence below is correct?

(A) Jon run in a race.

(B) Jon and May runs in a race.

(C) Jon and May run in a race.

4. Which sentence below is correct?

(F) I play with the truck.

(G) I plays with the truck.

(H) You plays with the truck.

Writer's Companion • UNIT 5
Lesson 5 *Writing Test Practice*

Name _____

C. For some questions, you will have to read a paragraph or passage. The sentences in those paragraphs or passages often are numbered. Remember to read the test tip. Answer the questions on the Answer Sheet below.

Read the passage. Then read each question and fill in the correct answer.

My Bunny

(1) Yesterday, I play with my bunny. (2) She ran around the house. (3) She jumped in the air. (4) I gave her an apple branch. (5) She like chewing on it. (6) Then she washed her face.

1. What change, if any, should be made in sentence 1?

A Change *play* to **plays**

B Change *play* to **played**

C Change *play* to **playing**

D Make no change

> **Test Tip:**
> Most verbs that tell about an action that happened in the past end with –ed.

2. What change, if any, should be made in sentence 3?

F Change *jumped* to **jump**

G Change *jumped* to **jumps**

H Change the period to a question mark

J Make no change

3. What change, if any, should be made in sentence 5?

A Change *like* to **liked**

B Change *chewing* to **chews**

C Change *chewing* to **chewed**

D Make no change

Answer all test questions on this Answer Sheet.

1. (A) (B) (C) (D)   3. (A) (B) (C) (D)

2. (F) (G) (H) (J)

D. On this test, you will have to read three sentences and
decide which is correctly written. Read the test tip.
Then answer the questions.

Read and answer questions 1–2. Mark your answers on the Answer Sheet.

1. Put the ideas in the box together to create a
sentence that makes sense.

> late yesterday, and
> late today.
> she is
> She was

Which sentence below correctly combines the
words from the box?

A She was late yesterday, and she is late today.

B She was she is late yesterday, and late today.

C she is late today. She was late yesterday, and

Test Tip:
The verbs *am, is,
are, has,* and *have*
tell about now.
The verbs *was,
were,* and *had* tell
about the past.

2. Put the ideas in the box together to create a
sentence that makes sense.

> a game soon.
> Ben have
> Luke and

Which sentence below correctly combines the
words from the box?

F a game soon. Ben have Luke and

G Ben have Luke and a game soon.

H Luke and Ben have a game soon.

© Harcourt

Answer all test questions on this Answer Sheet.

1. Ⓐ Ⓑ Ⓒ   2. Ⓕ Ⓖ Ⓗ

Name _____

Look at Exact Words

Time-order words help the reader understand the order in which story events happen. Exact **describing words** help the reader picture what is happening.

A. Read the following Literature Model. Look for time-order words and describing words.

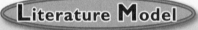
Literature Model

Today we're going to the park.

"*El parque es lindo,*" says Abuela.

I know what she means. I think the park is beautiful too.

"*Tantos pájaros,*" Abuela says

as a flock of birds surround us.

So many birds. They're picking up bread we brought.

—from *Abuela*
by Arthur Dorros

B. Identify time-order words and describing words.
1. Circle the word that tells the time the story begins.
2. Underline the words that describe what is happening.

C. How does the storyteller feel about the park? _____

_____

Name _____

Explore Exact Words

Writers use time-order words and other exact words to make their writing clear. They sometimes use verbs (action words) to describe exactly what is happening.

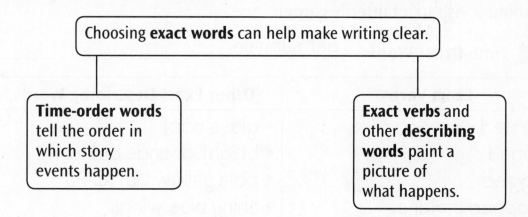

Choosing **exact words** can help make writing clear.

Time-order words tell the order in which story events happen.

Exact verbs and other **describing words** paint a picture of what happens.

A. Underline the time-order word or words in each sentence. Then put a box around the exact verb.

Example   Last week, I tiptoed into the baby's room.

1. Yesterday I grabbed a sock away from my dog.

2. This morning, my sister and I rushed out the door.

B. Read this sentence from *Abuela.* Underline the exact verbs.

We'd fly over factories and trains . . . and glide close to the sea.

C. Pretend that you were scared on a roller coaster. Write a sentence that describes what you did. Use an exact verb.

_____

_____

Name _____

Use Exact Words

Before you write a story, think about some of the words you will use. Make a list of time-order words and exact describing words to put in your story. Here is how one student writer planned a story about a visit to a butterfly garden.

Example **Time-Order Words:** _Last summer_

Exact Verbs	Other Exact Describing Words
• floated • sipped • giggled • snapped picture	• glass roof • bright orange butterfly • pale yellow butterfly • shiny blue wings

A. Think about something in your life to write about. List some time-order words and exact describing words you will use.

Time-Order Words: _____

Exact Verbs	Other Exact Describing Words

B. Now use words from your chart to write a paragraph about what happened. Use another sheet of paper.

© Harcourt

Name _____

The Parts of a Personal Narrative

In a **personal narrative,** a writer tells about something that happened in his or her life. Words such as *then, next,* and *last* help make the order of events clear. Here is a draft written by a second grader. As you read, think about how the student organized it. Then answer the questions.

Student Model

The Blue Butterfly
by Peter

Last summer, my aunt took me to see butterflies. They were in a building with a glass roof. Butterflies floated all around us. My favorite butterfly had shiny blue wings. We stood by some beautiful flowers. First, a bright orange butterfly sipped from a yellow flower. A pale yellow butterfly landed on a red flower. A striped butterfly sipped. The blue butterfly came. It sat on my head! I giggled, and my aunt snapped a picture.

> Use **time-order words** to tell the order in which things happened.

> Use exact **describing words** to give the reader a strong mental picture.

> Use **exact verbs** to help the reader picture what happened.

1. Find exact describing words that paint a picture of something. Underline them.
2. Find verbs that tell exactly what happened. Circle the verbs.

Writer's Grammar

In a personal narrative, writers use words such as *I, me, my, us,* and *we.* Find some of these words in the paragraph above.

Name _____

Evaluate a Personal Narrative

When you study a personal narrative, ask yourself these questions:

- Does the story have a beginning, a middle, and an end?
- Does the writer use time-order words to help the reader follow the sequence?
- Does the writer use exact words that give the reader a strong mental picture?

A. Reread the Student Model on page 161. Then answer the questions.

1. What time-order words tell when the story begins?

_____

2. What happens at the end of the story?

_____

3. What words give the reader a strong picture of the building?

_____

B. Now evaluate the Student Model. Put a check in the box next to each thing the writer has done well. If you do not think the writer did a good job with something, do not check the box.

☐ The story has a beginning, a middle, and an end.
☐ The writer used time-order words.
☐ The writer used exact words that paint a picture.

C. How do you think the writer could make the narrative better? Write your ideas below.

_____

See the rubric on page 207 for another way to evaluate the Student Model.

© Harcourt

Name _____

Revise by Adding Time-Order Words

One way the writer could make the narrative better is to add time-order words. Here is an example of a time-order word that could be added to the Student Model.

Example _Next_ , a pale yellow butterfly landed on a red flower.

A. Revise the Student Model by adding two time-order words. Use the Word Bank for ideas.

1. _____, a striped butterfly sipped.

2. _____, the blue butterfly came.

B. Revise the paragraph you wrote on page 160. Add time-order words. If you need more space, use another sheet of paper.

> **Word Bank**
> finally
> last
> now
> soon
> then
> _____
> _____

_____

_____

_____

_____

_____

_____

_____

_____

_____

_____

_____

© Harcourt

Writer's Companion • UNIT 6
Lesson 1 _Exact Words_

Name _____

Look at Putting Ideas in Order

A paragraph of information has an **introduction** and **details**. Details give information in an order that makes sense. Writers use time order, space order, or other kinds of order.

A. Read the following Literature Model. Find out how the details are organized.

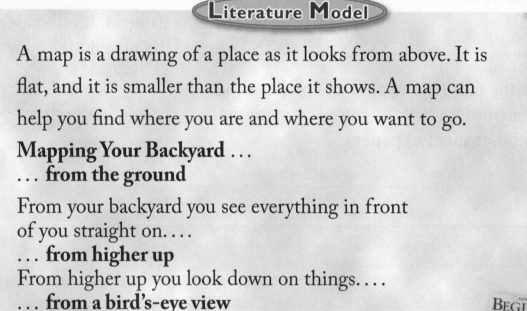

Literature Model

A map is a drawing of a place as it looks from above. It is flat, and it is smaller than the place it shows. A map can help you find where you are and where you want to go.

Mapping Your Backyard ...

... from the ground

From your backyard you see everything in front of you straight on....

... from higher up

From higher up you look down on things....

... from a bird's-eye view

If you were a bird flying directly overhead, you would only see the tops of things....

—from *Beginner's World Atlas*
National Geographic

B. Identify the introduction and sequence of details.
  1. Put a box around the introduction.
  2. The writer did not use time order to organize details. How are the details about mapping your backyard organized? Underline the words that show the order the writer did use.

C. Why does the order of details make sense? _____

_____

Name _____

Explore Putting Ideas in Order

Writers put details in an order that makes a paragraph easy
to understand. Sometimes writers put details in time order.
Sometimes writers use another kind of order.

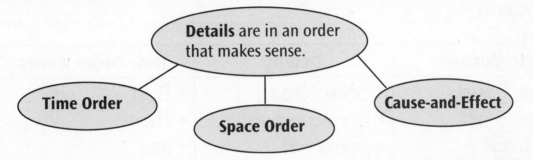

Details are in an order that makes sense.

Time Order

Space Order

Cause-and-Effect

A. **Put the details in a sequence that makes sense. Number the sentences 1,
2, and 3.**

Example __2__ Mom puts the leaves in large bags.

__1__ Mom rakes the leaves into piles.

__3__ A truck picks up bags of leaves.

1. _____ It snowed hard all night.

_____ Power came back at the end of the day.

_____ Wires were on the ground in the morning.

2. _____ Then the geese fly north in the spring.

_____ The geese fly south to a warm place.

_____ The geese gather at a pond in the fall.

B. **Read these sentences from *Beginner's World Atlas*. Put them back in the
sequence that makes sense.**

_____ You have to turn it to see the other side.

_____ You still can't see the whole Earth at one time.

_____ A globe is a tiny model of the Earth that you can put on a
stand or hold in your hand.

Name _____

Use Putting Ideas in Order

Sometimes writers put a paragraph in time order. They use time-order words to make the order clear. Here is how one student organized a paragraph about fossils.

Topic <u>Fossils</u>

Introduction	Details	Time-Order Words
• topic: fossils • what is left of things that lived long ago	• animal dies • buried in mud • parts rot • parts change to rock • fossils found	• first • then • next • after millions of years

A. Think of a topic you know about. Write the topic. Write down ideas for the introduction. Then list details and time-order words.

Topic _____

Introduction	Details	Time-Order Words

B. Now use information from your chart to write a paragraph about your topic. Do your writing on another sheet of paper.

© Harcourt

Name _____

The Parts of a Paragraph of Information

A **paragraph of information** has an introduction, details, and a conclusion. A **conclusion** summarizes or ends the paragraph. Here is a draft written by a second grader. As you read, think about how the student organized it. Then answer the questions.

Student Model

DRAFT

How Fossils Are Formed
by Ria

Fossils are what are left of things that lived long ago. First, a plant or animal that died was buried in mud. Some parts of it rotted away. After millions of years, scientists have found some of the fossils. Next, other parts of the plant or animal changed into rock. Fossils may be of plants or animals.

> Tell the topic in the **introduction** at the beginning of the paragraph.

> Give **details** that tell more information in the middle of the paragraph.

> Put the details in an order that makes sense.

> End the paragraph with a **conclusion.**

1. What is the topic of the paragraph? Circle it.
2. What detail tells what happened first to form a fossil? Underline it.
3. What time-order words did the writer use? Put a box around each one you find.

Writer's Grammar

Many verbs end with –d or –ed to tell about the past. Sometimes the letter before –ed is doubled. Find an example of a word that tells about the past in the paragraph above.

167

© Harcourt

Name _____

Evaluate a Paragraph of Information

When you study a paragraph of information, ask yourself these questions:

- Does the paragraph tell the topic in an introduction?

- Are the details in an order that makes sense?

- Is the paragraph written in a way that is interesting and easy to understand?

A. **Reread the Student Model on page 167. Then answer the questions.**

   1. What does the writer tell in the introduction?

   _____

   2. Is the paragraph easy to understand? Explain.

   _____

B. **Now evaluate the Student Model. Put a check in the box next to each thing the writer has done well. If you do not think the writer did a good job with something, do not check the box.**

☐ The writer told the topic in an introduction.
☐ The writer put the details in an order that makes sense.
☐ The writer wrote the paragraph in an interesting way.

C. **How do you think the writer could make the paragraph better? Write your ideas below.**

_____

_____

_____

_____

See the rubric on page 207 for another way to evaluate the Student Model.

© Harcourt

Name _____

Revise by Rearranging Details

One thing the writer of the Student Model could have done
better is put the details in time order. Here is an example of one
change in the order.

Example Move the sentence in dark type to the introduction:

Fossils are what are left of things

that lived long ago. **Fossils may**

be of plants or animals.

A. Revise the Student Model by organizing the details in time order.

   1. Add a time-order word to this sentence to help organize the details.
   Some parts of it rotted away.

   _____

   2. Which sentence should be moved to the conclusion?

   _____

   _____

   _____

B. Revise your paragraph on page 166. Move sentences so the order of
details makes sense. Add time-order words if you wish to help make the
order clear. Finish your writing on another sheet of paper.

_____

_____

_____

_____

_____

© Harcourt

Writer's Companion ▪ UNIT 6
Lesson 2 *Putting Ideas in Order*

Name _____

Look at Time-Order Words

Sometimes a paragraph gives steps that tell how to do or make something. The steps are in order.

A. Read the following Literature Model. Look for the steps that tell how to travel by train.

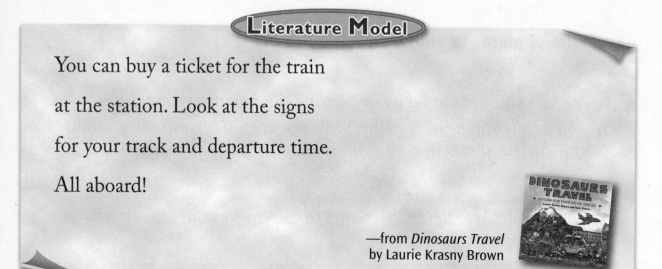

Literature Model

You can buy a ticket for the train

at the station. Look at the signs

for your track and departure time.

All aboard!

—from *Dinosaurs Travel*
by Laurie Krasny Brown

B. Identify the steps.
1. Circle the **first** thing you do to travel by train.
2. Underline the **next** step.
3. Put a box around the **last** step.

C. Where can a person buy a train ticket?

_____

© Harcourt

Name _____

Explore Time-Order Words

Steps are written in the order in which they need to be followed. **Time-order words** help show the sequence of the steps.

A **topic sentence** tells what your writing will explain.

Writing **steps in order** can help you organize your writing.

Time-order words help show the sequence of the steps.

A. A time-order word is missing from each sentence. Draw a line to show where each word belongs.

How To Make a Sea Mobile

Example First,————————paste a piece of string to each picture.
Next,————————cut out pictures of sea animals.
Last, —————————tie the pictures to a hanger.

How To Make a Paper Design

1. First,   open up the folded paper.
Next,   fold a square sheet of paper two times.
Last,   make little cuts on each folded side.

How To Play a Matching Game

2. First,   place all the cards face down.
Next,   keep the cards if they match.
Last,   turn over two cards.

B. Read this sentence. Then write time-order words to show the sequence of steps.

At the airport an agent looks at your ticket, checks
your bags, and then you take a seat on the plane.

_____, the agent looks at your ticket.

_____, the agent checks your bags.

_____, take a seat on the plane.

© Harcourt

Name _____

Use Time-Order Words

Before explaining how to do or make something, writers list the
steps in time order. They also list the things that are needed.
Here's how one student organized steps for making a bird feeder.

Example **Topic: How To** _Make a Bird Feeder_

Things Needed	Steps to Follow
• large pine cone • string • peanut butter • bird seed	1. Tie a string to large pine cone. 2. Put peanut butter on pine cone. 3. Roll pine cone in bird seed. 4. Hang feeder from branch.

A. Think about something you know how to do or make. Write down the
steps that tell what to do. Write the steps in time order.

Topic: How To _____

Things Needed	Steps to Follow

B. Now use information from your chart to write a paragraph about your
topic. Use another sheet of paper.

© Harcourt

Name _____

The Parts of a How-to Paragraph

In a **how-to paragraph,** a writer tells the things that are needed. Then the writer gives the steps to follow. Writers use time-order words to help show the order of the steps. Here is a draft written by a second grader. As you read, think about how the student organized it. Then answer the questions.

Student Model

Make a Bird Feeder
by Marcus

Here is an easy way to make a bird feeder. You need only a few things. Find a large pine cone. Get some bird seed and peanut butter. Tie a piece of string to the top of the pine cone. Next, put peanut butter on the pine cone. Then, roll the pine cone in the bird seed. Last of all, hang the feeder from the branch of a tree. Enjoy the birds that come to your feeder.

> Tell the topic in a **topic sentence.**

> Tell **things** that are needed.

> Write the **steps** in sequence.

> Use **time-order words** to help show the sequence of steps.

1. Underline the topic sentence.
2. Circle the three things the writer says you need.
3. What time-order words tell the last step? Put a box around them.

Writer's Grammar
A compound word is made up of two words that have been joined together. Some compound words, like *babysitter* or *thunderstorm*, are **closed** into a single word. Others, like *role-play*, are joined with a hyphen. Still others, like *high school*, are **open**, with a space in them. Find open compounds in the Student Model.

© Harcourt

Name _____

Evaluate a How-to Paragraph

When you evaluate a how-to paragraph, ask yourself these questions:

- Does the paragraph have a topic sentence?

- Does the paragraph tell all the things that are needed?

- Does the paragraph have time-order words that make the order of steps clear?

A. Reread the Student Model on page 173. Then answer these questions.

   1. What does the topic sentence say the paragraph will explain?

   _____

   2. What do the words *Then* and *Next* help show?

   _____

B. Now evaluate the Student Model. Put a check in the box next to each thing the writer has done well. If you do not think the writer did a good job with something, do not check the box.

☐ The writer told what the paragraph is about in a topic sentence.
☐ The writer told all the things that are needed.
☐ The writer told the steps in the order they should be done.
☐ The writer used time-order words.

C. How do you think the writer could make the paragraph better? Write your ideas below.

_____

_____

_____

© Harcourt

See the rubric on page 207 for another way to evaluate the Student Model.

Name _____

Revise by Adding Details

The writer of the Student Model could make the paragraph
better by adding some details. The writer could add another
thing that is needed and a time-order word. The writer could
make one step clearer. Here is an example of a detail that could
be added.

Example Get some bird seed and peanut butter.

Get some bird seed, peanut butter, and string.

A. Revise the Student Model by adding details. Write new sentences.

1. Add a time-order word:

Tie a piece of string to the top of the pine cone.

_____

2. Add words to make the step clearer:

Next, put peanut butter on the pine cone.

_____

B. Revise the paragraph you wrote on page 172. Add missing details.

_____
_____
_____
_____
_____
_____
_____

Name _____

Review Word Choice and Organization

Writers use **exact words** to describe story events. Writers also put events in some kind of order. Sometimes, writers use time order and time-order words in their writing.

A. Read the following Literature Model. Look for time-order words and exact describing words.

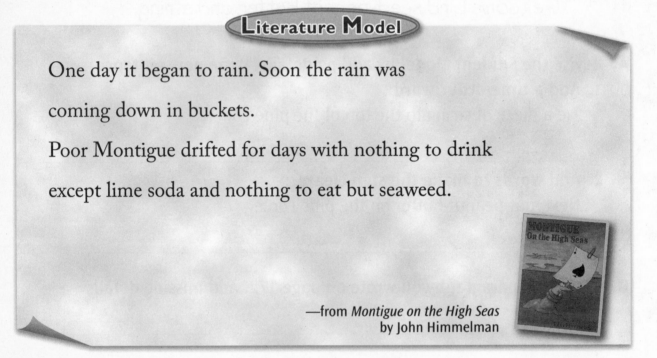

Literature Model

One day it began to rain. Soon the rain was

coming down in buckets.

Poor Montigue drifted for days with nothing to drink

except lime soda and nothing to eat but seaweed.

—from *Montigue on the High Seas*
by John Himmelman

B. Identify time-order words and describing words.
   1. Underline the words that tell when the story begins.
   2. Circle the time-order word that tells when the rain came down in buckets.
   3. Put a box around an exact verb in the last sentence.

C. Was there a lot of rain? Explain.

_____

_____

Name _____

Review Word Choice and Organization

Organizing details in **sequence** makes a paragraph easy to understand. Sequence is the order in which things happen.

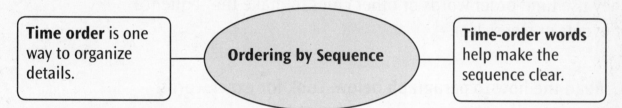

| **Time order** is one way to organize details. | **Ordering by Sequence** | **Time-order words** help make the sequence clear. |

A. Read this paragraph of information. Look at how the details are organized.

Sometimes new trees grow because of animals. In the fall, seeds fall from trees. Then, some seeds may stick to the fur of animals. Many animals carry the seeds to a new place. Next, the seeds fall off the animals and drop to the ground. After a while, trees may grow from the seeds.

B. Answer the questions about the order of details.

Example What is the first thing that happens to the seeds?

They fall from trees.
_____

1. What words tell when the first thing happens?

_____

2. What words tell what happens last?

_____

3. What other words help make the order of details clear?

_____

C. Write the last sentence with different time-order words.

_____

_____

Name _____

Review Word Choice and Organization

Writers use exact words to describe the details in a personal narrative, a paragraph of information, and a how-to paragraph. They use time-order words or other clues to make the sequence of events or steps clear.

A. **Read the how-to paragraph below. Look for exact words.**

You can make an elephant mask out of a paper bag. You will also need sheets of gray paper for ears and a trunk, scissors, paste, and a black marking pen. The first thing you do is cut holes for your eyes. Then, trace around the holes with the black pen. Next, draw and cut out big ears and a long trunk. Finally, paste the ears and trunk to the bag.

1. Write the words that describe these materials:

_____ bag

_____ paper

_____ marking pen

2. Write the time-order words that tell the steps.

_____

3. Write the verbs that tell exactly what to do.

_____

B. **Suppose you were writing a story about an elephant. Write two exact words to describe the way it moves its trunk.**

_____

_____

© Harcourt

Name _____

The Parts of Directions

When writing **directions,** a writer should number the steps to make the directions easy to follow. A writer should also use simple, clear language.

A. Below are directions written by a second grader. As you read, think about the words the writer uses to explain the steps. Then answer the questions.

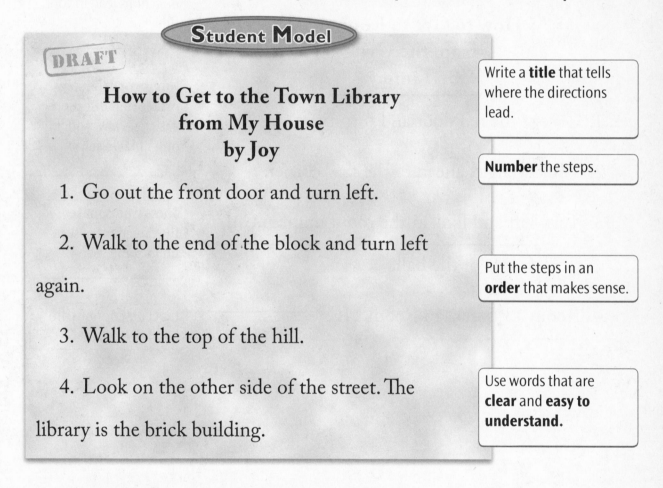

Student Model

DRAFT

How to Get to the Town Library from My House
by Joy

Write a **title** that tells where the directions lead.

1. Go out the front door and turn left.

Number the steps.

2. Walk to the end of the block and turn left again.

Put the steps in an **order** that makes sense.

3. Walk to the top of the hill.

4. Look on the other side of the street. The library is the brick building.

Use words that are **clear** and **easy to understand.**

1. Circle the simple verbs that tell what to do.
2. Underline the words in the second step that tell how far to walk.
3. Put a box around the exact words that describe the library.

Writer's Grammar
Most sentences in directions are commands. One sentence in the directions above is not a command. Find that sentence.

Writer's Companion • UNIT 6
Lesson 4 *Review Word Choice and Organization*

Name _____

Evaluate Directions

A. Two students wrote directions. The directions below got a score of 4. A score of 4 means excellent. As you read, think about the teacher's notes.

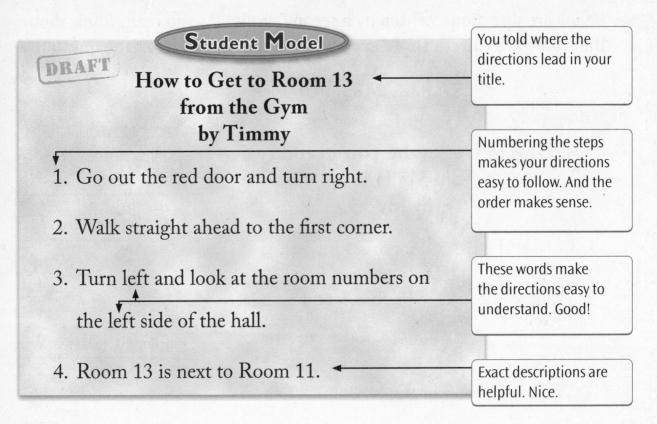

Student Model

DRAFT

How to Get to Room 13 from the Gym
by Timmy

1. Go out the red door and turn right.

2. Walk straight ahead to the first corner.

3. Turn left and look at the room numbers on the left side of the hall.

4. Room 13 is next to Room 11.

You told where the directions lead in your title.

Numbering the steps makes your directions easy to follow. And the order makes sense.

These words make the directions easy to understand. Good!

Exact descriptions are helpful. Nice.

Name _____

Evaluating the Student Model

B. This paragraph got a score of 2. Why did it get a low score?

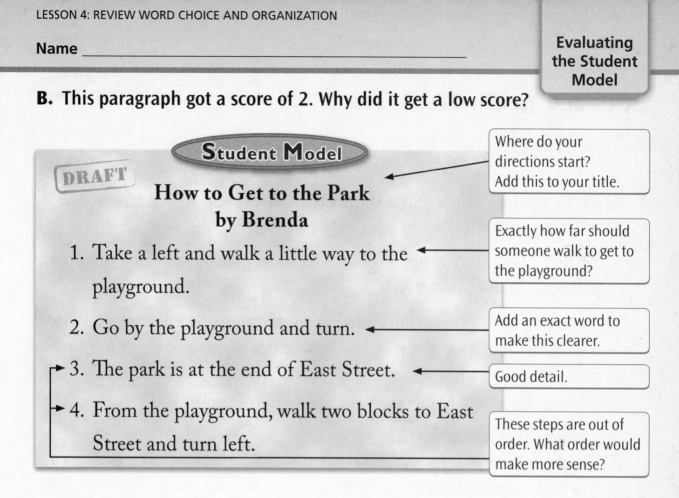

Student Model

DRAFT

How to Get to the Park
by Brenda

1. Take a left and walk a little way to the playground.

2. Go by the playground and turn.

3. The park is at the end of East Street.

4. From the playground, walk two blocks to East Street and turn left.

> Where do your directions start? Add this to your title.

> Exactly how far should someone walk to get to the playground?

> Add an exact word to make this clearer.

> Good detail.

> These steps are out of order. What order would make more sense?

C. What score would you give the student's story? Put a number on each line.

	4	3	2	1
Focus/Ideas _____	☐ The writing has a clear topic and main idea.	☐ The writing has a main idea.	☐ The topic and main idea are not very clear.	☐ There is not a clear topic or main idea.
Organization/ Paragraphs _____	☐ The writing tells ideas in order.	☐ The writing tells ideas in order most of the time.	☐ The ideas are not always in order.	☐ The ideas are not in order at all.
Word Choice _____	☐ The writing uses exact words and details.	☐ The writing uses some exact words and details.	☐ The writing uses only a few exact words.	☐ The writing does not use any exact words.

© Harcourt

Writer's Companion • UNIT 6
Lesson 4 *Review Word Choice and Organization*

Name _____

Extended Writing/Test Prep

On the last two pages of this lesson, you will write a longer piece.

A. **Read the choices below. Put a star by the writing you would like to do.**

1. Write about the following topic.

Writing Topic: Sometimes a ride is special. It may have been a ride in a car, bus, train, or plane.

Directions for Writing: Think about a special ride you have taken. Write a personal narrative about it. Use time-order words and describing words in your writing.

2. Choose one of the paragraphs you wrote in this unit:

- a personal narrative (page 160)
- a paragraph of information (page 166)
- a how-to paragraph (page 172)

Write another paragraph about the topic. Use what you know about exact words and sequence.

3. Write a new how-to paragraph. Use describing words and time-order words.

B. **Use the space below to plan your writing.**

TOPIC: _____

KIND OF WRITING: _____

WHAT WORDS WILL I USE: _____

_____

© Harcourt

Name _____

C. In the space below, draw a chart that will help you plan your writing. Fill in the chart. Write notes on the lines below.

Notes

_____

_____

_____

_____

_____

_____

_____

_____

D. Do your writing on another sheet of paper.

Writer's Companion • UNIT 6
Lesson 4 *Review Word Choice and Organization*

Name _____

Answering Multiple-Choice Questions

Some writing tests have questions with answer choices. This lesson will help you answer different kinds of questions often found in writing tests.

A. For some tests, you will have to read three sentences and decide which is correctly written. Read the test tip. Then answer the questions.

Read the questions below. Answer questions 1–4 on the Answer Sheet.

1. Which sentence below is correct?

A   Today, I sees a beautiful rainbow.

B   Yesterday, I see a beautiful rainbow.

C   Yesterday, I saw a beautiful rainbow.

2. Which sentence below is correct?

F   Tomorrow, Hank gave the dog a bone.

G   Now, Hank gives the dog a bone.

H   A week ago, Hank give the dog a bone.

3. Which sentence below is correct?

A   Visitors came here two days ago.

B   Visitors comes here two days ago.

C   Visitors come here two days ago.

4. Which sentence below is correct?

F   Earlier, Meg's cat run out the door.

G   Now, Meg's cat runs out the door.

H   Tomorrow, Meg's cat ran out the door.

> **Test Tip:**
> Verbs should help tell when something happened and should match the rest of the sentence:
> **Yesterday, I** *swam.*
> **Today, I** *swim.*
> **Tomorrow, I** *will swim.*

Answer all test questions on this Answer Sheet.	
1. Ⓐ Ⓑ Ⓒ	3. Ⓐ Ⓑ Ⓒ
2. Ⓕ Ⓖ Ⓗ	4. Ⓕ Ⓖ Ⓗ

Name _____

B. For some questions, you will have to read a passage. The sentences in the passage often are numbered. Read the test tip. Read the passage. Then read each question and fill in the correct answer on your Answer Sheet.

The Circus

(1) Last Saturday, my family went to the circus. (2) I always like the funny things the clowns does. (3) One clown put a banana under his hat. (4) Then he snapped his fingers and took off the hat. (5) The banana was gone! (6) I wonder how he doing that. (7) Where did that banana go?

1. What change, if any, should be made in sentence 1?

   A Change *went* to **go**

   B Change *went* to **goes**

   C Change *went* to **going**

   D Make no change

2. What change, if any, should be made in sentence 2?

   F Change *does* to **do**

   G Change *does* to **done**

   H Change *does* to **doing**

   J Make no change

> **Test Tip:**
> If an action takes place in the past, the verb should be in the past form, too. The verb in a sentence depends on who is doing the action. (I *make*; he *makes*)

3. What change, if any, should be made in sentence 6?

   A Change *doing* to **do**

   B Change *doing* to **did**

   C Change the period to a question mark

   D Make no change

© Harcourt

Answer all test questions on this Answer Sheet.

1. Ⓐ Ⓑ Ⓒ Ⓓ   3. Ⓐ Ⓑ Ⓒ Ⓓ

2. Ⓕ Ⓖ Ⓗ Ⓙ

Name _____

C. For some questions, you will have to decide the best way to write a sentence. Read the test tip. Then practice answering this kind of question on the Answer Sheet below.

1. What is the correct way to write the sentence?

   A   My brother and sister has build a toy castle for me.

   B   My brother and sister have built a toy castle for me.

   C   My brother and sister have build a toy castle for me.

   D   My brother and sister has built a toy castle for me.

2. What is the correct way to write the sentence?

   A   My sister have paint it pink.

   B   My sister has paint it pink.

   C   My sister has painted it pink.

   D   My sister have painted it pink.

> **Test Tip:**
> If you have time, quickly look over all the questions. Mark the answers you know. Then go back and do the others.

3. What is the correct way to write the sentence?

   A   I had always wanted a castle.

   B   I had always want a castle.

   C   I have always want a castle.

   D   I has always wanted a castle.

4. What is the correct way to write the sentence?

   A   We has been on vacation.

   B   We be on vacation.

   C   We have been on vacation.

   D   We has be on vacation.

Answer all test questions on this Answer Sheet.

1. Ⓐ Ⓑ Ⓒ Ⓓ   3. Ⓐ Ⓑ Ⓒ Ⓓ

2. Ⓐ Ⓑ Ⓒ Ⓓ   4. Ⓐ Ⓑ Ⓒ Ⓓ

© Harcourt

Name _____

D. For this test, you will have to pick a word that means the
same as the underlined phrase in a question. Read the test tip. Then
answer the questions.

Read the questions below. Answer questions 1–4 on the Answer Sheet.

1. What is the correct way to write the word that means <u>it is</u>?

   A its

   B its'

   C it's

   D i'ts

2. What is the correct way to write the word that means <u>were not</u>?

   A were'nt

   B weren't

   C werent'

   D wasn't

3. What is the correct way to write the word that means <u>not able to</u>?

   A can'not

   B cann't

   C can't

   D cant'

4. What is the correct way to write the word that
means <u>has not</u>?

   A have'nt

   B has'nt

   C hadn't

   D hasn't

Test Tip:
In a contraction,
one or more
letters are left out.
An apostrophe
takes the place of
the missing letters
(*did not—didn't*;
I am—I'm).

© Harcourt

Answer all test questions on this Answer Sheet.

1. Ⓐ Ⓑ Ⓒ Ⓓ   3. Ⓐ Ⓑ Ⓒ Ⓓ

2. Ⓐ Ⓑ Ⓒ Ⓓ   4. Ⓐ Ⓑ Ⓒ Ⓓ

Writer's Companion ▪ UNIT 6
Lesson 5 *Writing Test Practice*

Parts of Speech

The parts of speech are the different kinds of words you use in sentences.

Nouns are words that name people, places, or things.

> Person–The **conductor** shouts loudly.
> Place–We arrive in the **city.**
> Thing–The **train** stops moving.

Verbs show an action or tell what a person, place, or thing is like.

> We **walk** into the station.
> The room **is** very big.

The time a verb tells about is called its **tense.**

Present tense verbs tell about something that is happening now.

> Marta **visits** the city.

Past tense verbs tell about something that happened in the past.

> Marta **visited** the city last year.

Future tense verbs tell about something that will happen in the future.

> Marta **will visit** the city in June.

Pronouns are words that take the place of nouns.

> **Subject pronouns** take the place of nouns that name whom or what a sentence is about. *I, you, he, she, it, we,* and *they* are subject pronouns.
> > Carlos and **I** arrive. **We** see hundreds of people.

> **Object pronouns** take the place of nouns that receive the action of the verb. *Me, you, him, her, it, us,* and *them* are object pronouns.
> > Carlos stared at the people.
> > Carlos stared at **them.**

> **Possessive pronouns** show who or what has something. *My, your, her, his, its, our,* and *their* are possessive pronouns.
> > **His** eyes were wide with wonder.

© Harcourt

Adjectives are words that describe a noun or pronoun.

The **busy** crowds pushed past the **amazed** children.

Articles are special adjectives. *A, an,* and *the* are articles.

Use *a* before a noun that begins with a consonant.

Use *an* before a noun that begins with a vowel.

Use *the* before a specific noun.

We see **a** statue standing on **an** island New York Harbor. It is **the** Statue of Liberty.

Adverbs are also words that describe. Most adverbs describe verbs.

We **quickly** climb the steps in the statue.

Prepositions are words that connect a noun or pronoun to other words in a sentence. Here are some common prepositions.

above	after	at	before	by
in	near	of	on	out
to	over	under	up	with

We climb **to** the top. We gaze **over** the water. We look **at** the view.

Conjunctions are words that connect words or groups of words. *And, but,* and *or* are common conjunctions.

We see the whole city, **but** we also see New Jersey too.

Marta **and** Samuel point at the tall buildings.

© Harcourt

189

Sentences

A **complete sentence** is a group of words that tells a complete thought.

The children wait for the subway.
Watch out for that car!
Is the train coming yet?

The **simple subject** is the main word that tells what the sentence is about. It usually is a noun or pronoun.

The **tunnel** is dark.

The **simple predicate** is the main word that tells what is happening in the sentence. It is a verb.

Everyone **waits** quietly.

A **sentence fragment** is a group of words that does not tell a complete thought. To correct it and make it a complete sentence, you need to add a subject or a predicate.

FRAGMENT: The sound of the subway. (Needs a predicate.)
CORRECTION: The sound of the subway **is very loud.**

FRAGMENT: Squeals as it stops. (Needs a subject.)
CORRECTION: **The train** squeals as it stops.

A **run-on sentence** is a group of words that tells more than one thought. You can fix run-on sentences by breaking them into shorter sentences.

RUN-ON: We and our parents ate lunch then we went to see a show and we are getting tired now.
CORRECTION: We and our parents ate lunch. Then we went to see a show. We are getting tired now.

RUN-ON: We went to the biggest toy store in the world, it was amazing, you could get any toy you could ever imagine!
CORRECTION: We went to the biggest toy store in the world. It was amazing. You could get any toy you could ever imagine there!

© Harcourt

Combine sentences by putting together two or more sentences to make a longer sentence. Use the conjunctions *and, but,* or *or* to combine sentences.

CHOPPY: We tried to find our hotel. We were lost.
CORRECTION: We tried to find our hotel, but we were lost.

CHOPPY: We asked a police officer for help. He told us where to go.
CORRECTION: We asked a police officer for help, and he told us where to go.

Capitalization

Capitalize the first word in a sentence.

Snow fell during the night.

Capitalize nouns that name specific people, places, or things.

I ran to keep up with Marta.
We walked to Central Park.

Capitalize the pronoun *I*.

I thought the city looked beautiful.

Capitalize the names of streets, towns, cities, and states in addresses.

Our hotel was at 971 Park Avenue, New York, New York.

Capitalize the titles of people.

Mr. Murtha, the elevator operator, knew everyone.
He pointed to Mayor Green as he walked by.

© Harcourt

Punctuation

Use a **period** (.) at the end of a sentence that makes a statement.

It snowed all afternoon.

Use a **question mark** (?) at the end of a sentence that asks a question.

Can we have a snowball fight?

Use an **exclamation point** (!) at the end of a sentence that shows strong feelings.

Watch out for that snowball!

Use **commas** (,) to separate three or more items in a series.

We threw snowballs, made a snowman, and dug snow tunnels.

Use a **comma** to show a pause after an introductory word.

Hey, it is nearly lunchtime.
Samuel, put down that snowball!

Use a **comma** to join sentences using *and, but,* or *or.*

We went back to the hotel, and we had a big lunch.

Use **commas** between the name of a city and state in an address.

We told the waiter we were visiting from Taos, New Mexico.

Use **quotation marks** before and after a person's exact words.

"We love this city," Ellie said.

Use **quotation marks** around the title of a story, poem, song, or article.

The waiter taught us the words to the song "New York, New York."

An **abbreviation** is a shortened form of a word. It usually ends with a period.

Titles:	Mr.	Mrs.	Dr.	Jr.					
Days:	Mon.	Tues.	Wed.	Thurs.	Fri.	Sat.	Sun.		
Months:	Jan.	Feb.	Mar.	Apr.	Aug.	Sept.	Oct.	Nov.	Dec.
Streets:	St.	Ave.	Rd.	Dr.					
Times:	A.M.	P.M.	B.C.	A.D.					

© Harcourt

Usage

Plural nouns name more than one person, place, or thing. Make most nouns plural by adding -*s*.

> One **skater** bent to tie her skate.
> The **skaters** at Rockefeller Center twirled on the ice.

Add -*es* to make the plural of nouns that end in *s, sh, ch,* or *x*.

> We sat on a **bench** to lace our skates.
> The rink was lined with **benches.**

Change the *y* to *i* and add -*es* to make the plural of nouns ending in a consonant and *y*.

> I wondered what **country** the skater came from.
> We could see flags from many **countries** flying above us.

Change the *f* to *v* and add -*es* to make the plural of nouns ending in *f* or *fe*.

> We left our shoes on a **shelf** in the changing room.
> There were **shelves** full of shoes there.

Some nouns form their plurals in different ways. Here are some of them:

foot — feet	sheep — sheep	man — men
goose — geese	moose — moose	woman — women

Possessive nouns show who owns something. Use an **apostrophe** (') and -*s* to form the possessive of a singular noun.

> Marta**'s** feet were cold.

Use just an **apostrophe** to form the possessive of a plural noun that ends in -*s*.

> Our parents**'** faces were starting to look very tired.

Contractions are words made by joining two words and leaving out some of the letters.

> Samuel **didn't** want to go back to the hotel yet.
> **He'd** planned on seeing the Natural History Museum.

© Harcourt

In an contraction, use an **apostrophe** to replace letters that have been left out. Here are some common contractions:

I + am = I'm	she + will = she'll
we + have = we've	do + not = don't
he + is = he's	they + would = they'd

Subjects and verbs must agree in a sentence.

For singular subjects, use the singular form of a verb.

The taxi **stops** next to us.
The taxi **inches** down the street.

For plural subjects, use the plural form of a verb.

The cars **honk** at the taxi.

Adjectives and Adverbs can be used to compare people, places, and things.

Add -er to most short adjectives that compare two things.

New York City is much **bigger** than my hometown.

Add -est to most short adjectives that compare more than two things.

The Empire State Building is the **tallest** building I have ever seen.

Add more before longer adjectives that compare two things.

Fifth Avenue is **more beautiful** than any other street in New York.

Add most before longer adjectives that compare more than two things.

It was the **most exciting** place I have ever visited.

Add -er to most short adverbs that compare two actions.

People in New York City walk **faster** than anywhere else.

Add -est to most short adverbs that compare more than two actions.

We waited the **longest** time to get into the Natural History Museum.

Add more before longer adverbs that compare two actions.

We listened **more carefully** to the guide's talk than usual.

Add most before longer adverbs that compare more than two actions.

Our last day went by the **most quickly** of any other day.

© Harcourt

A **negative** is a word that has a meaning that is the opposite of a positive. Any contraction made with *not* is a negative. *No, not, none, no one, nobody, nothing,* and *never* also are negatives.

Use only one negative word in a sentence. Using two negatives is called a **double negative.** It changes the meaning of a sentence so that it says something you might not want to say.

> WRONG: We **don't never** want to leave the city.
> CORRECTED: We **don't ever** want to leave the city.
>   We **never** want to leave the city.

Irregular verbs are verbs that do not add *-ed* to form the past tense. You have to remember their spellings. Here are some common irregular verbs.

Present tense	Past tense
come (s)	came
do (es)	did
fall (s)	fell
give (s)	gave
have (has)	had
run (s)	ran
sing (s)	sang

Tricky Words

Homographs are words that are spelled the same but have different meanings. Sometimes they are pronounced differently. Here are some common homographs:

ball	bat	bound	can	close
date	dove	fair	fan	fit
fly	kind	left	ring	saw

Homophones are words that sound alike but have different spellings and different meanings. Here are some common homophones:

be/bee	bare/bear	blue/blew	by/buy
eye/I	knew/new	Maine/mane/main	road/rode/rowed

To figure out the meaning of homographs and homophones, read the sentence carefully. Think about the possible meanings of each homonym or homophone. Then decide which meaning makes the most sense. If you aren't sure, look up the word in a dictionary.

> HOMONYM: As the train doors **close,** we squeeze **close** together.
>> Meaning 1 of **close:** come together
>> Meaning 2 of **close:** near or tightly

> HOMOPHONE: We **rode** the train home and soon arrived at our own **road.**
>> Meaning of **rode:** to be carried or moved
>> Meaning of **road:** a paved path for cars

© Harcourt

Spelling Tips

When you are not sure how to spell a word, these tips can help.

- Remember how to spell most words with *i* and *e* together by using this rhyme:

  I before *e*
  Except after *c*
  Or when sounded like "ay"
  As in *neighbor* or *weigh*.

fi**e**ld	chi**e**f
ceiling	re**ce**ive

- A word with a long vowel sound often has a silent *e* at the end.

can**e**	tim**e**	pol**e**	cub**e**

- When a word ends in a silent *e,* drop the e to add *-ed* or *-ing.*

  pil**e** – pil**ed**   hav**e** – hav**ing**

- When a short word has one short vowel and one short consonant, double the consonant to add *-ed* or *-ing.*

  pl**an** – pla**nned**   h**it** – hi**tting**

- When a word ends in a consonant and *y,* change the *y* to *i* to add *-ed* or *-ly.*

  c**ry** – cr**ied**   happ**y** – happ**ily**

- When a word ends in *ie,* change the *ie* to *y* to add *ing.*

  d**ie** – d**ying**   l**ie** – l**ying**

There are some words that are similar in spelling to other words. Knowing their meanings will help you use them correctly.

- **it's:** the contraction of *it is.* **It's** fun to visit New York City.
  its: the possessive form of it. The Big Apple is **its** nickname.

- **lay:** *to put.* We **lay** the suitcases on the floor.
  lie: *to rest flat.* I **lie** across two seats to take a nap.

- **their:** the possessive form of *they.* Some people have lost **their** tickets.
  they're: the contraction of *they are.* **They're** looking everywhere for them.

- **to:** *in the direction of.* The train is taking us back **to** Taos.
  too: *also.* Other people are going there, **too.**
  two: the number after *one.* I have **two** bags of presents.

- **your:** the possessive form of *you.* **Your** friends will like the gifts.
  you're: the contraction of *you are.* **You're** going to miss the city!

Proofreading Strategies

Our language follows **conventions,** or rules. We write in sentences. We end them with punctuation marks. We leave spaces between words. We indent paragraphs. All of these conventions help people understand what we write.

As you proofread your writing, you should check to make sure you have followed the conventions. These strategies will help you proofread:

Wait before proofreading.

Put your writing away for a while. Then come back to it. You may see new things.

Proofread in steps.

1. Look at your **sentences.** Are they complete? Are they written correctly? Are your **paragraphs** indented?
2. Check your **language use.** Do your subjects agree with your verbs? Have you used the correct forms of adjectives and adverbs? Have you followed the rules for **capitalization** and **punctuation?**
3. Last, check your **spelling.** Circle any words that look strange. Use a dictionary if necessary.

Proofread with a partner.

Two pairs of eyes are better than one. Your classmate may find mistakes you did not see.

Proofreading Checklist

This checklist will help you as you proofread your work.

Sentences and Paragraphs

☑ Is every sentence complete?

☑ Does each sentence begin with a capital letter and end with the correct end mark?

☑ Is each paragraph indented?

Grammar and Usage

☑ Do your verbs agree with their subjects?

☑ Have you used *I* and *me* correctly?

☑ Have you used the correct form of adjectives and adverbs that compare?

Capitalization and Punctuation

☑ Have you capitalized proper nouns and the pronoun *I*?

☑ Have you used commas, quotation marks, and apostrophes correctly?

Spelling

☑ Are you sure of the spelling of every word?

☑ Have you always used *there* and *their* correctly?

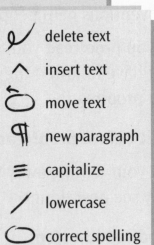

ℓ/	delete text
∧	insert text
↻	move text
¶	new paragraph
≡	capitalize
/	lowercase
◯	correct spelling

© Harcourt

Presenting Your Work

Sometimes you write for yourself. Most of the time, you write for other people. When you let other people read or hear your writing, you **publish** your work.

You can publish your writing in many ways. Here are some ideas.

Publishing Ideas for Any Type of Writing

- Read your writing aloud.
- Have a friend read it silently.
- Post it on a bulletin board.

Publishing Ideas for Descriptions and Poems

- Draw or paint a picture to go with your writing.
- Cut pictures from a magazine. Make a collage.
- Make up a dance to go with your writing.
- Find a piece of music to go with your writing. Make a tape recording in which you read while the music plays in the background.

Strategies Good Writers Use

- Use your best handwriting.
- Add drawings that help your readers understand and enjoy your writing.

Publishing Ideas for Stories

- Work with friends. Act out your story.
- Draw pictures to go with your story.
- Read your story aloud to another class.
- Make a class storybook.
- Send your story to a magazine.
- Mail your story to a relative far away.

Acting Out a Story

You can follow these steps to perform a story or a personal narrative.

Step 1

Plan how the people in your story should sound. What are their voices like? How do they say their words?

Step 2

Find props for your story. You can use different kinds of clothing, pictures, and other things.

Step 3

Decide how you want to present your story. Do you want to read it just as it is written, or do you want act it out? You could even ask classmates to help you present your story as a play.

© Harcourt

Publishing Ideas for Reports

- Add maps and pictures. Make a tabletop display.
- Make a poster for the classroom bulletin board.
- Teach your classmates about your topic.
- Put your report in the classroom library for others to read.

**Strategies
Good Writers Use**

- Give your work a title.
- Put your name on your work.
- Check your facts and proofread carefully before you send a letter in the mail or post work on a website.

Giving an Oral Report

Strategies	Applying the Strategies
Make note cards.	• Write each main idea on a note card. Put your cards in order, and number them.
Practice.	• Give your talk to a friend or family member. Think about how to make your talk better.
Speak clearly and slowly.	• Speak more slowly than you do when you're just talking. Look at your audience. Remember that they can learn from you.

Strategies for Listeners

- Think about the speaker's main idea.
- Try to learn from what you hear.
- Ask questions to learn more.

Writer's Glossary of Terms

adjective: a word that describes a noun

adverb: a word that describes a verb, an adjective, or another adverb

detail: a fact, event, or statement; details usually tell about a main idea

dialogue: words spoken by characters in a story or play

directions: writing that tells how to do something

fact: something that is true

friendly letter: a letter written to someone you know

how-to paragraph: a paragraph that tells how to do something

letter: a written message to someone

letter of invitation: a letter asking someone to come to an event

main idea: what something is mostly about

paragraph: a group of sentences with a single main idea or topic

paragraph that describes: a paragraph that tells what something or someone is like

paragraph that gives information: a paragraph that presents facts and data

paragraph of explanation: a paragraph that tells how something works or what something is like

personal narrative: a story about the experiences of the writer

personal story: a story about what happened to the person who wrote the story

poem: a piece of writing, often with rhyme

predicate: what the subject of a sentence does or is like

reason: why something happens or is true

research report: a piece of writing that comes from study and from looking things up

rubric: a guide for scoring or evaluating something

sequence: the order in which things happen

subject: what a sentence is about

topic: what something is about

verb: a word that names an action

		Score of 4 ☆☆☆☆	Score of 3 ☆☆☆	Score of 2 ☆☆	Score of 1 ☆
FOCUS/IDEAS		The topic of my story is very clear.	The topic of my story is clear.	The topic of my story is not so clear.	The topic of my story is not clear at all.
ORGANIZATION/ PARAGRAPHS		My story tells the events in the correct order. My paragraphs are indented and my story is finished.	My story tells the events in order most of the time.	Events are not told in order in some places.	My story does not tell the events in order at all.
DEVELOPMENT		My story uses time-order words to tell the events in the correct order.	My story uses time-order words to tell the events in the correct order most of the time.	My story needs more time-order words to show the order in which events happened.	My story does not use time-order words.
VOICE		My writer's voice is very clear.	My writer's voice is clear.	My writer's voice is not very clear.	My writer's voice is not clear at all.
WORD CHOICE		I use describing words and details to tell the story.	I use some describing words and details to tell the story.	I need more describing words and details.	I do not use describing words or details.
SENTENCES		I use different kinds of sentences. My sentences are complete.	I use different kinds of sentences some of the time. Most of my sentences are complete.	I need to use different kinds of sentences. Some of my sentences are not complete, or they are too long.	I use the same kind of sentence for the whole story. Some of my sentences do not make sense.
CONVENTIONS		I use capital letters and commas correctly. All of my words are spelled correctly.	I use capital letters and commas correctly most of the time. Most of my words are spelled correctly.	I use capital letters and commas correctly some of the time. Some of my words are spelled correctly.	I use capital letters and commas incorrectly. A lot of my words are spelled correctly.

Writer's Companion
Student Rubrics

	FOCUS	ORGANIZATION	SUPPORT	CONVENTIONS
Score of 6 ☆☆☆☆☆	My writing has a clear main idea. It has enough detail sentences to explain the main idea.	I use time-order words to tell the events or ideas in the correct order. My paper seems complete.	I use clear details that help explain the main idea. My words are exact.	I use different kinds of sentences. All of my words are spelled correctly. My sentences are complete. Nouns and verbs are used correctly. Capital letters and commas are used correctly.
Score of 5 ☆☆☆☆	My writing has a main idea. It has some detail sentences to explain the main idea.	I use some time-order words to tell the events or ideas in the correct order.	I use details that help to explain the main idea. Most of my words are exact.	I use different kinds of sentences. My words are spelled correctly. My sentences are complete. Nouns and verbs are used correctly most of the time. Capital letters and commas are usually used correctly.
Score of 4 ☆☆☆	My writing has a main idea. It needs more detail sentences to explain the main idea.	I need to use more time-order words to tell the events or ideas in the correct order. My writing does not seem finished.	I use some details that help to explain the main idea. Some of my words are exact.	I use some different kinds of sentences. Most of my words are spelled correctly. Most of my sentences are complete. Nouns and verbs are used correctly most of the time. Capital letters and commas are used correctly most of the time.
Score of 3 ☆☆	My writing has a main idea. It needs detail sentences.	I need time-order words to tell the events or ideas in the correct order. My writing does not seem finished.	I use a few details that help to explain the main idea. A few of my words are not very clear or exact.	Most of my sentences are alike. Some of my words are spelled correctly. Most of my sentences are complete. Some of my nouns and verbs are used correctly. Capital letters and commas are sometimes used correctly.
Score of 2 ☆☆	The main idea is not clear. It needs detail sentences.	I do not tell the events or ideas in the correct order.	I need more details to explain the main idea. My words are not very clear or exact.	Most of my sentences are alike. Only a few of my words are spelled correctly a few of my sentences are complete. A few of my nouns and verbs are used correctly. Sometimes, I use capital letters and commas correctly.
Score of 1 ☆	My writing does not have a main idea.	My writing is not finished.	I use no details to explain the main idea. My words are not exact.	My sentences are not complete or are all the same. Most of my words are not spelled correctly. I do not use nouns and verbs correctly. I do not use capital letters and commas correctly.